Trip Around the World

A Country Quilt Block Travelogue

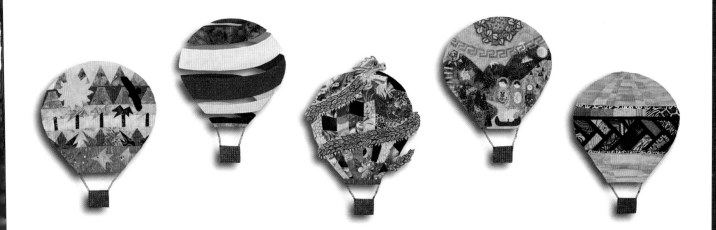

Holly Anderson & Anita Zaleski Weinraub

Photography by Tucker J. H. Bair

Editorial Assistance from Stephanie Weinraub

An offering of the Georgia Quilt Project, Inc.

Schiffer Publishing Ltd

4880 Lower Valley Road, Atglen, Pennsylvania 19310

Dedication

We dedicate this book to the people of the world, in celebration of our diversity as well as our sameness. All people, regardless of race, culture or socioeconomic status can find the common ground that we all dearly crave but that all too often proves elusive in the face of conflict. It comes down to simply being *human*; we all have the same basic needs of food, clothing, and shelter; we are members of families; we love our children. This human condition is universal and is not limited or changed by borders between countries.

"Cover" Wall Hanging
Design by Holly Anderson, Helga Diggelmann, and Anita Zaleski Weinraub. Individual balloons made by (from left to right) Anita Zaleski Weinraub, Helga Diggelmann, Ben Hollingsworth, Debra Steinmann, and Nicole Blackwell. Top pieced and appliquéd by Holly Anderson. Machine quilted by Sue Hunston. Embellishments include crystals, beads, inkwork, hand painting, and threadwork. The undulating landscape at the bottom was inspired by a traditional quilt block and the colors of the arcs are those of the Olympic rings, a nod to the Georgia Quilt Project's Gift of Quilts to the 1996 Centennial Olympic Games. 43" x 54", cotton.

Other Schiffer Books on Related Subjects:
Fiber Expressions: The Contemporary Quilt. Quilt National. ISBN: 0887400930. $12.95
Heirloom Quilt Designs for Today. Lorie Martin & Jim Burnley. ISBN: 9780764326691. $24.95
New Quilts. Nancy Rae. ISBN: 0887401570. $14.95
A Quilt Block Challenge: Vintage Revisited. Mary Kerr. Foreword by Pepper Cory. ISBN: 9780764334573. $24.99
Quilting Traditions: Pieces from the Past. Patricia T. Herr. ISBN: 0764311212. $29.95
Quilts: The Fabric of Friendship. The York County Quilt Documentation Project & The York County Heritage Trust. ISBN: 0764311956. $29.99

Designed by Mark David Bowyer
Type set in Florens LP / Lydian BT

ISBN: 978-0-7643-4000-0
Printed in China

Schiffer Books are available at special discounts for bulk purchases for sales promotions or premiums. Special editions, including personalized covers, corporate imprints, and excerpts can be created in large quantities for special needs. For more information contact the publisher:

Published by Schiffer Publishing Ltd.
4880 Lower Valley Road
Atglen, PA 19310
Phone: (610) 593-1777; Fax: (610) 593-2002
E-mail: Info@schifferbooks.com

For the largest selection of fine reference books on this and related subjects, please visit our website at **www.schifferbooks.com**
We are always looking for people to write books on new and related subjects.
If you have an idea for a book, please contact us at
proposals@schifferbooks.com

This book may be purchased from the publisher.
Include $5.00 for shipping.
Please try your bookstore first.
You may write for a free catalog.

In Europe, Schiffer books are distributed by
Bushwood Books
6 Marksbury Ave.
Kew Gardens
Surrey TW9 4JF England
Phone: 44 (0) 20 8392 8585; Fax: 44 (0) 20 8392 9876
E-mail: info@bushwoodbooks.co.uk
Website: www.bushwoodbooks.co.uk

The Itinerary

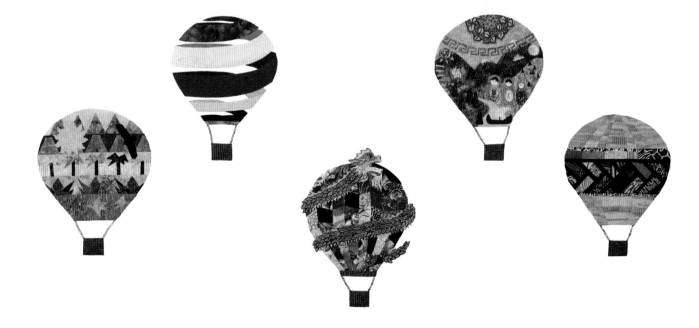

✓ Pre-flight Instruction

C lose your eyes and think for a moment about the countries of the world. Imagine the diversity within those countries—the richness of different landscapes—mountains, deserts, rainforests, plains, beaches, even cities. Now layer on top of this geographic panorama the myriad cultures of the world. Culture doesn't have to mean "ethnicity"—in fact, it defies definition. It is comprised of such small things as what clothes we wear, what stories we tell, what customs and traditions we cling to, and what your momma served you for dinner each night. Your culture can be a business suit or a sarong; mac n' cheese or a samosa; Kokopelli or Baba Yaga. In this book, more than 150 people have come together to showcase this wealth of global diversity by compiling the world's most comprehensive collection of quilt blocks representing the countries of the world. All you need do is flip through the pages of this book to enjoy the result! Treat yourself and absorb the incredible variety of blocks created by our artist/quilters—each block is an exquisite work of art. As the saying goes, "it takes a village," and we have indeed drawn upon the talent of our quilting "village" to create this powerful collection. Come away with us, take a deep breath, and immerse yourself in a delightful journey of discovery.

Origins of the Project

The country block project was conceived and begun in 1996, when Atlanta was in the midst of hosting the Centennial Olympic Games. Under the auspices of the Georgia Quilt Project, Georgia's quilt makers had stitched more than 500 quilts, which were given to team representatives at both the Olympic and Paralympic Games, a gift from Georgia's quilt makers to the people of the world. At that time, the Georgia Quilt Project invited each quilt maker to create a 12" quilt block representing the country that had received his/her quilt. About seventy of the Olympic quilt makers chose to participate. Their blocks were mounted and displayed at the Uniform Distribution Center in Decatur, Georgia, where all Olympic volunteers and staff picked up their uniforms during the spring and early summer prior

to the Games. After the Olympics and Paralympics, the country block project was tabled and the partial collection stored to be taken up at another time.

Fifteen years later (!), the blocks were re-examined; the decision was made that they should not be wasted and should be shared with the world. The project was revived.

Nuts and Bolts

The rules were simple: a quilt maker had to pledge to make a block, then make a choice from the list of available countries. Blocks were to be of original design, 12" finished size, any technique, any fabric, any kind of embellishments, with finished edges on any appliqué. The country's flag could not appear on the block—we did not want 207 blocks of flags! Participation was not limited to the Olympic or Paralympic quilt makers—anyone with a tie to Georgia could make a block, or more than one. Block makers were asked to submit an artist statement along with their blocks. In determining which countries to include, our decision was based on whether they were sovereign states and also whether they sent a team to the Olympic Games. Puerto Rico and Guam, for instance, are not sovereign states but do have Olympic teams. Conversely, Vatican City does not have an Olympic team but is a sovereign state. Surprisingly, or perhaps not, there were some "new" countries on the list that did not exist in 1996 (East Timor, South Sudan, and several former Yugoslavian republics) as well as a couple that no longer exist (Zaire, Yugoslavia). We have been as careful and inclusive as possible when compiling our list of countries. Any errors or omissions are entirely our own with no intent to offend.

Off and Running

The revival of the project was immediately met with enthusiasm by Georgia's quilt makers and soon the first of the "new" blocks arrived. Some quilters chose to create a block that represented a country familiar to them or to which they had some tie or personal connection (Congo, Latvia, Liberia, Ireland, St. Kitts and Nevis, and Moldova come to mind); others specifically chose a country that was new to them. All were eager to begin learning about "their" country and figure out just the right way to represent it in cloth.

Our Block Makers

As mentioned above, anyone with a tie to Georgia was eligible to make a block. Our block makers are primarily residents or former residents of Georgia. They vary in age from their twenties to their eighties and include two men. They are all quilt makers, some nationally known professionals who have won many prizes for their work, others fairly new to quilting. Their occupations are as varied as the blocks they created—stay at home moms, retirees, teachers, small business owners, a flight attendant, attorneys, physicians, an arts administrator, a professor or two, and a banker. They are cancer survivors, volunteers, singles, moms, dads, widows, a widower, grandmas, grandpas, and even great grandmas, and a great grandpa! An asterisk after a block maker's name indicates that he or she made an Olympic or Paralympic quilt.

Presenting ... the Blocks!

The blocks are as varied and diverse as the countries they represent and the people who made them. Each is unique, but there are characteristics that some have in common. Many, many block makers chose to use the colors of the country's flag in their blocks, since we discouraged depicting the flag itself. And many of those colors were used in a creative, sometimes subtle way (Equatorial Guinea, Sweden). Sometimes the colors of the flag were used in the background of the block, with a superimposed motif (Andorra, Belarus, Cameroon, Estonia). Several block makers began with a traditional quilt pattern and then reinterpreted it in the context of their block design (Egypt—moon over the mountain, Mozambique—snail's trail, Zambia—log cabin).

The differences between the blocks made in '96 and those made in 2010 and 2011 are striking, though neither group is more beautiful or impressive than the other. The blocks made fifteen years ago tend to be more traditional. Only one early block contains any embellishment (Guatemala). Not so today! Today's quilters use a wide variety of threads and embellishments of all kinds to enhance their work. In our blocks you will find threadwork (Belize, Indonesia), painting (American Samoa, Chile, Guyana, Niger), inkwork (Canada), beading (India, Nigeria), crystals (Nigeria, Sudan), metal (Spain), spangles (Brazil), yarn (Eritrea), stenciling (Jordan), stamping (Burundi), pen and ink (Bolivia, Senegal), hand embroidery (India, Sri Lanka), machine embroidery (Italy, St. Kitts and Nevis), purchased appliqués (Vanuatu), shells (Micronesia, Niger), photo transfer (Afghanistan, Ireland, Israel, Malaysia, USA), yo-yos (St. Vincent and the Grenadines), and dimensional appliqué and folded work (Dominica, Micronesia, Spain). [The countries appearing in parentheses are not necessarily the only examples of the technique described.]

The Internet was in its infancy back in '96; nobody could research their countries on the web. By contrast, almost all of the recent block makers made use of the Internet to learn about their countries. A surprising amount of research was done, as quilters looked for that one photo or tidbit of information that resonated with them and inspired them in making their blocks.

Care in choice of fabrics is another characteristic that jumps out. Quilters have more fabrics available to them now than ever before and our artists put them to excellent use in the blocks. Architectural, sky, sea, tree, mountain, animal, and earth fabrics abound and enrich the landscapes and seascapes our artists portray. Cotton is the predominant fabric choice (especially batiks!), but lamé (Belgium, Palestine), upholstery cloth (South Sudan and Sudan), polyester (Papua New Guinea), cotton flannel (China), and silk (Nigeria) found their way into the blocks. Several blocks incorporate fabric from the country depicted (Australia, New Zealand) or fabrics that evoke the country or continent (Botswana, Mozambique).

Many appliqué techniques appear in the blocks, from the most exquisite needle turn (Japan, Kazakhstan, North Korea) and reverse appliqué (Cook Islands) to stained glass (Algeria) and several kinds of fusible appliqué, finished by straight stitch, buttonhole stitch, zigzag or other decorative stitches (Singapore). Some blocks combine appliqué and piecing (Chile, Sweden).

Even though great conflicts and wars are taking place in some parts of the world, the artists chose more universal themes to represent the countries. This sensitivity on the part of the block makers reinforces our belief that a country and its people are more than just the latest occurrences on the political front and speaks to the desire of the makers to represent timeless rather than transient themes in their blocks.

Particular attention should be paid to the artist statements—we guarantee that you will learn things about the countries of the world that you did not know! Even the artist statement about a block as seemingly obvious and recognizable as the Eiffel Tower (France) will widen your knowledge—did you know that it was originally painted RED??? Did you know that butterflies swarm in the Central African Republic, or that Uzbekistan is one of the world's foremost exporters of cotton? Be sure to scrutinize the artist statements, both for the artist's interpretation to better understand the block and to enhance your knowledge. Just as we stated when making the Olympic quilts, we firmly believe that becoming more familiar with the ways of the peoples of the world can lead to greater understanding among all people and, ultimately, to world peace. A lofty goal, but nevertheless this project is one tiny, "quilty" step toward bringing people together.

Not only do we learn about some of the differences among the countries of the world through an examination of the blocks and the artist statements, but we also see similarities as well. What is more universal than women speaking to each other on their way to shop—at the mall or the market place (Chad, Somalia, South Sudan)? Or people decked out in traditional finery for a celebration (Dominica, Eritrea, Niger, Philippines)? Flowers are decorative motifs in many cultures and appear in several blocks (Czech Republic, Paraguay, Syria).

Block Arrangement

Rather than simply portray the blocks alphabetically, we present them here divided into their sections of the world, roughly corresponding to the continents. Within each section, they appear alphabetically. This gives the reader an inkling of how the different sections of the world "look," gives some organization to the collection, and makes the 207 blocks more manageable.

Cover Wall Hanging

To introduce each section, the balloon from the cover wall hanging corresponding to that section is presented in close-up, along with the artist's explanation of his or her balloon. From the intricate detail in the Europe balloon, to the wispy, ribbon-like Asia balloon, each balloon sets the "mood" of its section and invites the reader to explore further.

The Blocks and YOU

You, the reader, can use the blocks in this book in many different ways. Keep in mind that the blocks are merely one person's vision of a country. It's possible that while you study the blocks, another interpretation of a country will spring to your mind ("I would have done THIS."). Go for it! We hope that the blocks will serve as a jumping-off point for you to explore your own creativity, as well as a source of inspiration for you to create something of your own either based on or inspired by the blocks.

A wall hanging of "My Caribbean Cruise," "My African Safari," "My Roots," or "The Places I'll Go," which highlights the appropriate blocks and unifies them, perhaps through color selection, is an excellent way to use the blocks in this book. Different settings can show off the blocks as well. Rather than placing your blocks in a traditional setting of rows with sashing in between, perhaps linking your blocks with a meandering "yellow brick road" of your own creation would highlight them to greater advantage. Or borrow from the St. Kitts and Nevis block and frame each of your blocks in a circular frame, as if viewed from the porthole of a cruise ship. Or create a diamond-shaped or other shaped frame. An African safari quilt can have varying beiges to represent desert sand, interspersed with "oases" borrowed from some of our tropical island blocks. Africa's savannahs and jungles can also be created with elements from other blocks.

We encourage readers to make a personalized balloon with elements meaningful to them and create a small wall hanging (a balloon template can be found as a free download on the Georgia Quilt Project's website). When repeated, several of the pieced blocks form secondary patterns and would make interesting wall hangings or quilts. Adding a border or two in colors that will make the block "pop" is a perfect way to achieve a pillow-sized piece.

Several blocks act as a template of sorts for you to customize the block and make it your own. The United States block comes to mind, where your own photos can be substituted to create a block of your own, filmstrip style. That's pretty straightforward, yet still a creative way to highlight your photos of a vacation, family reunion, wedding or other event you would like to commemorate in cloth. Instead of an event, consider using photos of your family or best friends to create a lasting memory.

Take a look at the Cameroon and Andorra blocks—their "template" involves a traditional background block superimposed with figures in silhouette. The possibilities here are many—pick your favorite traditional block, make it in your favorite colors, and then personalize it with silhouettes that are meaningful to you. These background blocks can also be made in the colors of a university or high school team. Silhouettes can be any kind of sport, activity, animal, flower, or person, and any color can be used—they don't have to be in the traditional black! This is a concept that would lend itself particularly well to a fund-raiser quilt for a school sports team, or a treasured quilt for a child, a grandchild or a grandmother.

How about borrowing the "negative space" concept from the Yemen block and "writing" your favorite saying or short poem with this method? Or just your name? Or a friend's name?

Picking and choosing elements from different blocks and combining them is another way to make a block of your own. Pick your favorite palm tree, match it up with your favorite beach hut, find some luscious sea and sky fabrics (so many available these days), add your own embellishments, whether they be sea shells, flip-flops, sand pails or a tall glass of a tropical beverage, and you've just designed your own "beach block." Combine some of our castles or other architectural motifs and design a block of an imaginary land or of places you would like to visit.

Making a block and framing it as a gift for an international friend or a friend who has a connection to that country is a simple yet meaningful project. One way to frame the blocks is to first mount them on a square of stiff interfacing, turning under the 1/4" seam allowance. This gives a nice finished edge. From there, the block can be mounted on a stretched canvas (available at arts and crafts and/or artists' supplies stores). By not encasing it under glass the texture of the fabric and embellishments can more easily be seen and appreciated. A block or blocks can be similarly mounted and made into a wall piece to highlight your family heritage. Mounting the blocks in a traditional frame with an acid-free mat under low-glare uv-protected glass will protect them better from dust, light, and people's urges to touch them, however, so it is up to you!

Using the blocks as a teaching tool is another way to make them work for you. The book can give children ideas for researching and creating their own designs for country blocks—and not necessarily in fabric. Country blocks can be painted, pasted up with construction paper, drawn, etc. Doing research and learning about another country and culture while letting imaginations soar are the goals; this book can serve as a starting point in a classroom, with a scout troop, at a summer camp, or in helping your children or grandchildren to come to a better understanding of their world.

The Georgia Project has produced a series of patterns based on some of the blocks for those who would like more specific directions to follow. Ask for them at your favorite quilt shop or order them from our website. Whether you design your own country blocks, or make a balloon, or make a wall hanging based on the country blocks in this book, please send us via email pictures of your creations! We promise to post as many as possible on our website in order to share and perhaps give further inspiration to fellow quilt makers. We can't wait to see what you come up with—it will be a thrill for us to see what projects our country blocks have inspired.

What's Next?

The Georgia Quilt Project will display the blocks as a collection at many venues during 2012 and beyond. We are committed to sharing the talent of our quilt makers with the world. Both the travel schedule of the blocks, as well as ordering information for the patterns and the free balloon template, are available on our website: www.georgiaquiltproject.com. Check the website from time to time for updates as display schedules in particular can change. More information about the Georgia Quilt Project can be found there too.

Prepare for Takeoff

Now that you have completed your pre-flight instruction, it is time to take off and experience the breadth and depth of the world's countries as depicted in cloth by quilt makers. We begin with the Americas, which stretch from the Arctic to the Antarctic. Most of the countries therein, however, are clustered between the tropics of Cancer and Capricorn and enjoy a tropical climate. Among the countries of the Americas are many popular tourist destinations and you will find yourself longing to be on one of those beaches enjoying the sparkling waters!

Asia will follow—it spans almost half the globe and encompasses many cultures, religions, and climates. From the steppes of Russia and Mongolia to the steamy Indian subcontinent, Asia's diversity is mind-boggling!

Fly on with us to the next destination—Southeast Asia, Oceania, and Western Pacific Rim! Old and new cultures collide and mix here. We have countries with tropical climes, exotic tourist destinations, all steeped in tradition.

Europe is what many of us think of as the "Old World." Indeed, there are many relics and reminders of Europe's rich history depicted by the artists.

Africa has some of the oldest cultures on our planet, as well as unique and abundant wildlife. Its natural beauty, its stark and unforgiving deserts along with its savannahs and ubiquitous sunshine are reflected in its blocks.

An exhilarating visual feast is in store for you as you turn the next pages and begin your "trip around the world." Up, up and away we go!

AMERICAS BALLOON—Anita Zaleski Weinraub*, Atlanta, Georgia

"Mountains form the spine of the Americas, from Alaska to Patagonia. The Mesoamerican pyramids represent the native cultures and the red background alludes not only to their practice of human sacrifice, but also to bloody conflicts with Spanish conquistadors. Most of the countries in the Americas fall between the Tropic of Cancer and the Tropic of Capricorn and, by definition, enjoy a tropical climate. I adapted the palm tree from several depicted in the Americas' country blocks, and the lush vegetation in the penultimate row is a mini version of the Costa Rica block. Lastly, the abundance of life 'under the sea' is represented by a fish, borrowed from the Cayman Islands block. An Incan sun shines over all and a condor (California? Andean?) soars effortlessly along the thermals of its native land. In this way, I created a 'sky to sea' balloon to represent the Americas."

ANTIGUA AND BARBUDA—Therese Bocchino, Duluth, Georgia

"There are 365 beaches on Antigua, one for every day of the year! Barbuda has shell-laden beaches that stretch for miles. The constant trade winds make these islands ideal for yacht cruising and racing. I relied on these facts to create my vision of Antigua and Barbuda."

ARGENTINA—Diane Knott, Cumming, Georgia

Argentina evokes memories of rolling green hills, wineries, free grazing cattle, wide blue skies, and beautiful people. Also famous for its music, its dancing, and its amazing food, the spirit of Argentina remains with every visitor. The colors of the Argentinian flag form the background and an appliquéd silhouette of tango dancers in the center of this star block.

ARUBA—Lindsay Moss* and the Georgia Friendship Quilters*

"The blue represents the crystalline waters of the Caribbean, the green represents the lush foliage and plant growth. Gold is found in both the flag of Aruba and its coat of arms."

BAHAMAS—Maria Chisnall*, Nassau, Bahamas

"A line from the national anthem of the Bahamas inspired this block: 'Lift up your head to the rising sun, Bahamaland'!"

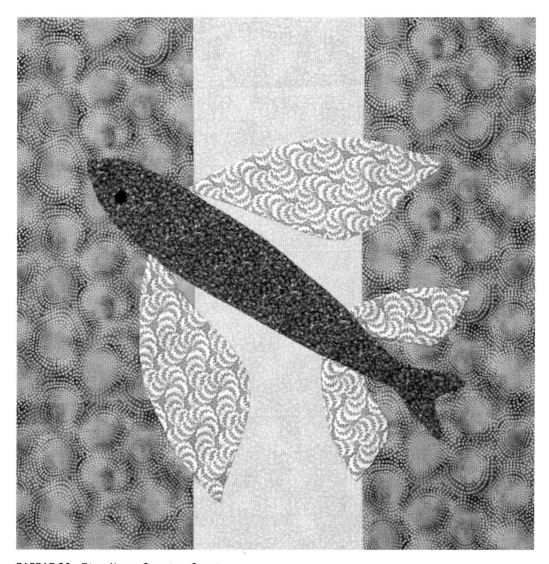

BARBADOS—Diane Knott, Cumming, Georgia

"Barbados uses the colors of the sun and sea in its flag, so I chose those for my background. I added a flying fish because it is the national 'dish' of the island. I love the beauty of the beaches, the sunsets, and the amazing array of wildlife that lives among the people of the island."

BELIZE—Carolina Fuchssteiner, Snellville, Georgia

"I have two passions—quilting and sailing in the Caribbean, so putting my passions together in this block was easy! To me, the 'blue hole' is a magical place. This is my interpretation of the 'blue hole' as seen when approaching Belize by air."

Bermuda

BERMUDA—Carole Helper*, formerly of Macon, Georgia

"The star in the center represents the warm, friendly people of Bermuda. Light pink is the color of the sand on Bermuda's beaches. A traditional 'ocean waves' pattern surrounds the central motif, echoing the beautiful waters around the island. The stars in the outer border fabric represent the many other 'stellar' qualities of the islands— botanical gardens, underground caves, flourishing sea life, unique architecture, golf courses, and so many other things!"

BOLIVIA—Sally Mitchell, Atlanta, Georgia

"Llamas
High, Andes mountains
Breathtaking panoramas
Heart and hardworking, hat-wearing people
A stunning country."

BRAZIL—Melinda Rushing, Atlanta, Georgia

"One of the symbols that best characterizes Brazil is the exuberant revelry of the pre-Lenten celebration of 'Carnival', a four-day extravaganza marked by parades of costumed dancers and musicians, formal balls, street dancing, and musical contests—a truly national party during which Brazilians briefly forget what they call the 'hard realities of life'. Through the use of costume—notably called 'fantasia' in Portuguese—anyone can become anybody at carnival time. Class hierarchies based on wealth and power are briefly set aside, poverty is forgotten, and Brazilian society blends in a dizzying blaze of color and music."

BRITISH VIRGIN ISLANDS—Holly Anderson*, Cumming, Georgia

"I admit it: I'm a beach bum! The image of this tropical Caribbean paradise brings to mind lazy days on the beach, reading, day dreaming or building sand castles. Also known as a mecca for sailors, it's clear why the British Virgin Islands, with their friendly people, favorable trade winds, and temperatures that vary only about ten degrees from winter to summer, are such a popular tourist destination."

Canada

CANADA—Holly Anderson*, Cumming, Georgia

"Used everywhere from its flag to hockey uniforms, the iconic red maple leaf has become synonymous with all things Canadian. Standing tall, acting as the stem of the leaf, is a totem, a traditional native Canadian wooden sculpture used to depict legends, family lineage or notable events. Some say the top figure is the most important, where others claim the opposite. In any event, it is the origin of the saying, 'low man on the totem pole'!"

19

CAYMAN ISLANDS—Sue McCranie*, Willacoochee, Georgia

"This block is a simple nine-patch design, easy to piece and requires only two fabrics—one for the fish and one for the water. The pristine waters surrounding the Cayman Islands contain a wealth of marine life; snorkeling and scuba diving are popular activities among the tourists visiting these beautiful islands."

CHILE—Cindy Rounds Richards*, Snellville, Georgia

"My niece's Chilean husband, Andrés, loves to camp and fish when he goes home to visit his family in Santiago. The center of the traditional Delectable Mountains block is the 'Cuernos del Paine' or 'The Horns', which I painted with tsukineko inks. I used a striped fabric to encircle the mountains to show that the national flower, the Copihues, is a vine. The Copihues petals appliquéd in the corners curl up showing a spotted underside, which I accomplished with a dimensional petal."

COLOMBIA—Jan Antranikian, Alpharetta, Georgia

"When I think of Colombia, I think of my morning cup of coffee, one of that country's foremost exports. Mountains in the background (where that little red bean grows so well!), a bag of beans, and a cup in the foreground make me think about brewing up my favorite Colombian blend!"

COSTA RICA—Carla Zahl Jolman*, Muskegon, Michigan

Bromeliad of Costa Rica

"A Central American country, Costa Rica has shorelines on both the Caribbean and the Pacific. Tropical terrain and lush tropical flowers were the ideas that prompted the design. The block was foundation paper pieced."

23

CUBA—Danielle Throneberry, Nashville, Tennessee

"I studied in Cuba for six magical weeks while in college. The country always evokes memories of crystal blue skies, old buildings, mountains covered in trees, and ceramic tile. This block was created using Two Star Design die-cut fusible shapes and machine appliqué."

Dominica

DOMINICA—Belinda Pedroso, Atlanta, Georgia

"I enjoy creating! This lady is all adorned in her traditional Dominican cultural dress. I personally want my quilt art and quilt works to reflect the authenticity of people as they share their culture through fabric."

Dominican Republic

DOMINICAN REPUBLIC—Ray Barreras, Atlanta, Georgia

"Thousands of humpback whales migrate to the Dominican Republic's Samana Bay every year to breed. Protection laws to ensure the safety of this endangered species are strict. The Samana Bay sanctuary is one of the world's largest. It is also one of the world's best places to whale-watch. My whimsical whale depicts the importance of the Dominican Republic's gentle waters in preserving this important mammal."

ECUADOR—Melinda Rushing, Atlanta, Georgia

"About half of all breeding pairs of blue-footed boobies make their home on Ecuador's Galapagos Islands. The male boobies take great pride in their fabulous feet and during mating rituals they show them off to prospective mates with a high-stepping strut. The bluer the feet, the more attractive the mate! Recalling the comical antics of these birds when I visited the Galapagos Islands inspired this block."

EL SALVADOR—Terri McGhee Jarrett, Nicholson, Georgia

"In creating my block, I decided to focus on El Salvador's abundant natural beauty by depicting a tropical flower. The bright colors and movement represent the vibrancy and dynamism of the rich culture. The petals of the flower are intended to resemble flames, and represent the volcanoes found in the country."

GRENADA—Deborah Risberg, Alpharetta, Georgia

"Grenada is universally known as the 'Spice Island'. The nutmeg tree grows profusely throughout the island. It is a symbol of the island's bounty and as such it is found on the country's coat of arms as well as its flag. The island's 7000 nutmeg farmers produce approximately one quarter of the world's supply. For these reasons, I decided to use this spice to represent Grenada."

Guatemala

GUATEMALA—Pat Schumacher*, Lawrenceville, Georgia

"In 1996, my Olympic quilt was given to Guatemala, so I was thrilled to have the opportunity to re-engage with this country by participating in this country block project! Although surrounded on both sides by ocean, Guatemala itself is quite mountainous, so I decided to depict the stunning contrast between the breathtaking mountains plunging down to the blue sea below."

GUYANA—Patsy Eckman*, Cumming, Georgia

"Since I have a special affinity for frogs, the Golden Frog of Guyana came to mind. It spends its whole life in the bromeliads of the rain forests of that country. I hand painted my frog, and placed him in his native tropical surroundings."

HAITI—Jan Antranikian, Alpharetta, Georgia

"Haiti shares the island of Hispaniola with its neighbor to the east, the Dominican Republic. Many species of tropical flowers and animals thrive here. Pictured in my block is the Hispaniolan Trogon, Haiti's national bird. Its ideal habitats are the moist subtropical or tropical mountainsides, where it requires a cavity of a large tree in which to nest. Threatened with extinction due to extensive deforestation, the Trogon has shown signs of adapting and can now be found at higher altitudes in the forests of Haiti's mountain ranges."

HONDURAS—Pat Kramer, Lawrenceville, Georgia

"I printed onto fabric a photo of the Mayan ruins of Copan, as well as the macaw, a native bird of Honduras. The leaves, stones, etc. are raw-edge appliqué. Embellishments include Swarovski crystals, three-dimensional flowers, and thread. I have traveled to Honduras several times to bring supplies to and teach women how to make useful objects they can sell in order to supplement their incomes."

JAMAICA—Cynthia Millar*, Roswell, Georgia

The friendliness and exuberance of the Jamaican people come across clearly in this block! This Jamaican lady sports a halo of sunshine, and her earrings allude to the rich musical traditions and the dynamic, popular urban recording industry of Jamaica. Reggae, ska, mento, rocksteady, dub, and other musical genres originated here. The red background evokes the vibrancy of life in this Caribbean island.

Mexico

MEXICO—Melinda Rushing, Atlanta, Georgia

"One of the world's smallest dogs, the Chihuahua is thought to have originated centuries ago in Mexico—after all, there is even a state of Chihuahua in Mexico. Treated as a sacred dog and even thought to help passage into the afterlife, the Chihuahua has always been a significant part of the family. A friend's Chihuahua, Peanut, inspired the coloring of the one portrayed. A sombrero and a cactus in the background further identify this block as ¡México!"

NICARAGUA—Deborah Raptis, Dahlonega, Georgia

"The bright colors used by Nicaraguans in their native costumes inspired this sea turtle. Floating on a background of tranquil, crystalline water (Pacific? Caribbean?), my turtle was embellished with machine and hand embroidery, and beadwork."

Panama

PANAMA—Sandy Myers*, Gainesville, Georgia

"To me, Panama brings to mind turquoise water, tropical flowers, and lush green mountains. I chose a 4-patch configuration because it reflects the Panamanian flag. The star patches are pieced with tropical floral and shrimp prints, alternating with crazy patch representing the wonderful, lush mountains."

PARAGUAY—Holly Anderson*, Cumming, Georgia

"'Mburucuyá' or the passion fruit flower, is the national flower of Paraguay. Sometimes referred to as the 'Maypop', its fruit is used to make juice, ice cream, and other tasty desserts. It's even used in medicines that aid in the treatment of bronchitis and asthma. I used dimensional appliqué with thread embellishments to portray this beautiful flower."

PERU—Sally Schuyler*, Atlanta, Georgia

"My block reflects the Incan worship of the sun (center portion of the block), the mountainous terrain (black and white), and the flag, which is stripes of red, white, and red with the national crest in the central white stripe."

PUERTO RICO—Maru Mattimoe, Atlanta, Georgia

"Photographer Jani Patokallio captured this iconic guerite of Fort San Felipe del Morro on the most northwesterly point of Puerto Rico. Like Megatron, I transformed his photo into a block using hand appliqué and methods learned from a class taught by Ellen Apte."

St. Kitts and Nevis

ST. KITTS AND NEVIS—Rosalind Rubens Newell, Lithonia, Georgia

"This block was made using Sharon Schamber's Piec-liqué technique. It features Mount Liamuiga, the highest peak on the island. It also shows the playful African Green Vervet monkey, which was introduced to the two-island nation in the past and has become naturalized there. The warmth of the sun is shining down on residents and visitors alike. If you approach St. Kitts and Nevis by cruise ship, your view may look like this—through a porthole! I particularly wanted to make this block because my great grandparents, Olive Grimes and Hezekiah Brown, emigrated from St. Kitts to New York City in the early 1900s."

ST. LUCIA—Carolina Fuchssteiner, Snellville, Georgia

"St. Lucia is an island of tropical rainforests, waterfalls, and the beautiful twin Pitons depicted here, which literally tower over the beach and plunge into the sea. Breathtaking!"

ST. VINCENT AND THE GRENADINES—Maxine Rounds Moore, Lawrenceville, Georgia

"A nation of thirty-two islands located in the Lesser Antilles of the Caribbean, St. Vincent, and the Grenadines' flag is represented by the use of the blue found in the sky and sea. The yellow is for the warmth of the yo-yo sun, the sand, and the people; the green represents the lush vegetation of the landscape. The colorful birds perched above the verdant landscape recall St. Vincent's annual Carnival celebration, called *Vincy Mas*. Construction methods include Sharon Schamber's 'Piec-liqué' technique, along with machine embroidery, Broderie Perse appliqué, and hand-stitched yo-yos. Don't miss the appliquéd surfer dude, complete with dreadlocks!"

Suriname

SURINAME—Jan Antranikian, Alpharetta, Georgia

"Despite being the smallest country in South America, Suriname has a full range of geographic features—mountains, savannahs, and beaches along the Atlantic coast. It's quite tropical and I wanted to represent its national flower, the Faja Lobi (Passion Love Flower) in my block."

TRINIDAD AND TOBAGO—Jul Kamen*, Georgetown, Texas

My Island Home

"For a small island country, Trinidad and Tobago has a wealth of diverse architectural styles. Spanish, French, Moorish, Indian, and British influences have resulted in Neoclassical, Victorian, and even Art Deco examples in public buildings and private estates. In this block, I have chosen to portray the most basic of all styles, a traditional rural East Indian house built of mud and roofed with palm leaves. Oh, the simple life!"

UNITED STATES OF AMERICA—Anita Zaleski Weinraub*, Atlanta, Georgia

"Reproducing photos taken on a cross-country trip onto fabric (with help from Joe Bautsch), I have created a film-strip style block highlighting many famous U.S. landmarks—the Statue of Liberty, Mt. Rushmore, the Grand Canyon, and the Golden Gate Bridge. Partially visible are some buffalo, Harkness Tower in New Haven, Connecticut, and the Pacific Coast. The block was adapted with permission from the 'Picture This' pattern, designed by Karen Montgomery of The Quilt Company of Allison Park, Pennsylvania. Anyone can use vacation photos, family photos or even squares of fabric (think fussy-cut!) with this format to achieve a lively and personal result. The 'roadmap' background fabric was a fortuitous find and adds a nice touch! I dedicate this block to the memory of Elaine Ratiner who had originally pledged to make the USA block, but who lost her battle with cancer before she was able."

U.S. VIRGIN ISLANDS—Marge LaBenne*, Hendersonville, North Carolina

"The three main islands of the U.S. Virgin Islands are surrounded by the blue/green waters of the Caribbean. St. Croix is red/yellow representing the colonial forts and town. St. Thomas has a beautiful blue harbor and sand beaches. St. John has a lush green National Park."

URUGUAY—Priscilla Casciolini*, Grayson, Georgia

"Uruguay is a land of gauchos, grasslands, cattle, beaches, rivers, and amethyst mines. The gaucho hat I designed reflects these elements and is a pieced nine-patch design with a little bit of appliqué."

VENEZUELA—Karen Byers, Tucker, Georgia

"This is my interpretation of the famous Angel Falls, surrounded by lush, tropical mountains. I love creating things, especially from fabric, needle, and thread. This was my first attempt making a landscape block—I enjoyed the challenge and was pleased with the result."

ASIA

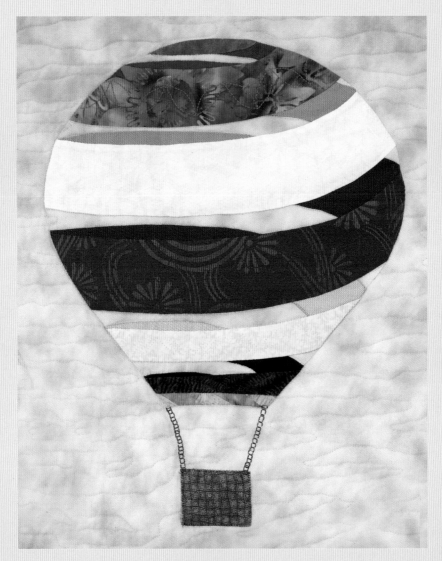

ASIA BALLOON—Helga Diggelmann, Alpharetta, Georgia

"The countries of Asia, though connected at their borders, are separated by distinct cultures, languages, political, and faith systems. What they have in common is that throughout history most of them have been linked by one or more trade routes, e.g. the tea route, spice route, silk road, incense route as well as the trans-Siberian railway.

My Asia balloon is a representation of the separate nations traversed and linked by the trade routes. It incorporates the colors in the Asian flags more or less proportionately, and the stitching is stylized representations of the four most common themes in the nations' coats of arms—flora, birds, celestial bodies, and horses."

Afghanistan

AFGHANISTAN—Claudia Lilly, Marietta, Georgia

"These children, dressed in traditional Pashtun costume, took part in the celebration of the opening of a new wing at a girls' school in Kabul. The delight on the faces of the children captured my heart, and I wanted them to be the centerpiece of my block. The Blue Mosque in Northern Afghanistan provides the background—its twin blue domes are one of Afghanistan's most iconic sites." *Photo of children by Capt. Robert Romano, US Army.*

Armenia

ARMENIA—Nancy Sohl* and the Cumming Sunset Quilters*, Cumming, Georgia

"Though it is a small, landlocked country, Armenia contains within its borders a variety of landscapes including barren plains, rain forests, snow-capped peaks, and alpine lakes. The strong lines and bold, contrasting colors represent the resilience and perseverance of the Armenian people. I chose the mountains of Armenia to reinforce this idea of endurance, and cast them in the colors of the Armenian flag."

Azerbaijan

AZERBAIJAN—Teddy Pruett, Lake City, Florida

"Azerbaijan sits atop land filled with natural gas and oil. 'Azer' means fire. Thousands of years ago, inhabitants who worshipped fire built Fire Temples in which natural gas came from the ground and burned through all four corner chimneys and the center of the building. The practice died out with Christianity, but many temples remain as testimony to this 'land of fire'. The crescent moon and eight-pointed star are elements taken from Azerbaijan's flag."

Bahrain

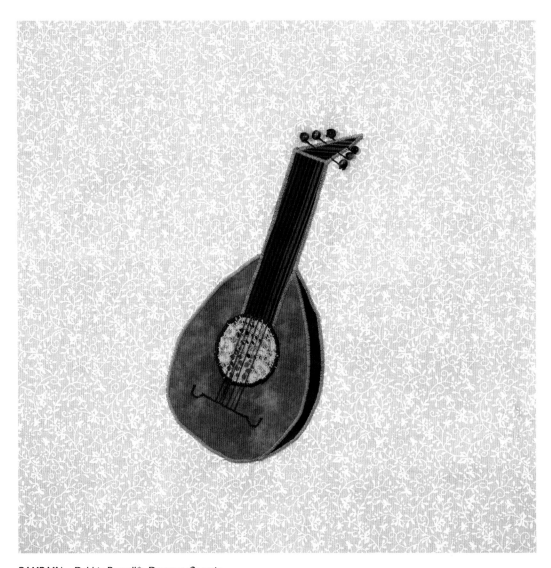

BAHRAIN—Debbie Russell*, Decatur, Georgia

"The oud is a pear-shaped instrument commonly used in Middle Eastern music. It is an ancestor of the lute, though it lacks frets and has a smaller neck. The music of Bahrain is elaborate and repetitive, following the traditional Arabic mode. It is typically played on the oud."

Bangladesh

BANGLADESH—Irma J. Young, Jonesboro, Georgia

"I was fascinated to read about rickshaw art when researching Bangladesh. This 'people's art' is frequently inspired by movie posters and the cinema culture, and has its creative roots in Bengali folk art. Boys, beginning as young as ten, are trained in this art form. There are more than 700,000 pedal rickshaws in Bangladesh, and more than 90% are decorated. I chose a colorful fabric for my rickshaw, and cut a round piece of lace in half to create the wheels."

Bhutan

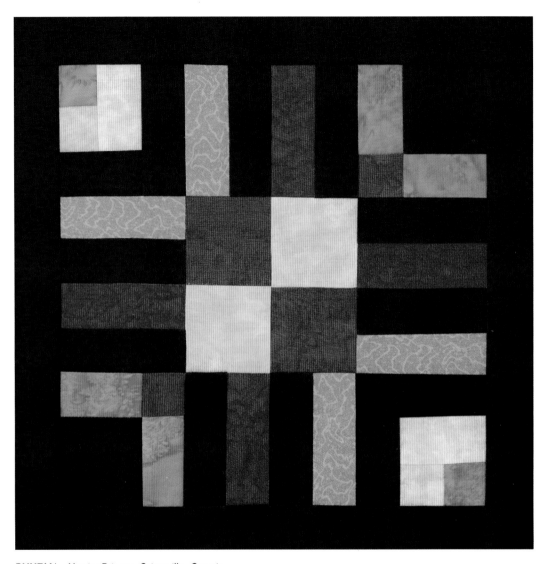

BHUTAN—Harriet Briscoe, Gainesville, Georgia

The inspiration for this block was a Bhutanese tapestry. The crisp, bright colors and geometric design result in a pleasing pieced block that would lend itself well to repeating in a quilt or wall hanging.

China

CHINA—Melinda Rushing, Atlanta, Georgia

"Dragons are legendary creatures in Chinese mythology and folklore, symbolizing potent and auspicious powers, particularly control over water, rainfall, and floods. The Chinese people take their dragons very seriously; I'll never forget the high rise hotel at Repulse Bay, Hong Kong, that was built with a hole in the middle of it. The architect had consulted a Feng Shui expert because apparently legend has it that a dragon lives in the mountain behind the hotel and in order to keep him happy, the building was designed with a huge hole that allows the dragon to get to and from the sea!"

Georgia

GEORGIA—Priscilla Ordway, Roswell, Georgia

"According to mythology, Colchis, on the Black Sea, was the site where Jason found and retrieved the Golden Fleece. This is just one part of Georgia's long and fascinating history."

India

INDIA—Judy Bush*, Ellenwood, Georgia

"I chose to design and sew the India block because my Olympic quilt went to India. When I think of India, I think of exotic, rich fabrics with gold embellishments. My block style, crazy patch, originated in the Victorian era and is one of my favorites. Batik fabric seemed to represent India perfectly to complete the project."

IRAN—deigned by Ann J. Taylor*, Gainesville, Georgia; made by Holly Anderson*, Cumming, Georgia

Stitched in rich golds, reds, and blues, this block's design was inspired by a Persian rug. Geometric and symmetrical, the simple square and triangle shapes are arranged here in a central medallion style, with three borders that set it off perfectly.

Iraq

IRAQ—Pomelia Wasdin, Conyers, Georgia

"In designing this block, I looked for symbols associated with Iraq. The block was inspired by a beautiful Islamic tile that depicted this white flower. The flower has many petals on top of lovely blues and greens. I intentionally used colors that were *not* brown or tan like the Iraqi desert because someday soon I hope Iraq will be restored to peace and beauty, just like the flower on the tile."

ISRAEL—Linda Christensen, Atlanta, Georgia

"The Hoopoe was recently (2008) chosen as Israel's national bird because its ability to find insects with its long beak enables it always to survive, just as the people of Israel have survived over the years. I just love the coloring and the perfect black polka dots on the bird's crest. The photo transfer was embellished with inkwork." *Photo by Sylvain Hellio of Natural Visions, used with permission.*

Jordan

JORDAN—Sandy Henry*, Dahlonega, Georgia

"These clay pots are examples of some of the indigenous pottery of Jordan. The stenciled motifs are typical of designs that can be found on jugs, pots, and other pottery for sale in the markets throughout the country."

Kazakhstan

KAZAKHSTAN—Gail Oliver, Roswell, Georgia

"This design represents the ornate embroidery found on Kazakhstan's traditional costumes in the distinctive golden yellow and sky blue colors of the national flag."

Kuwait

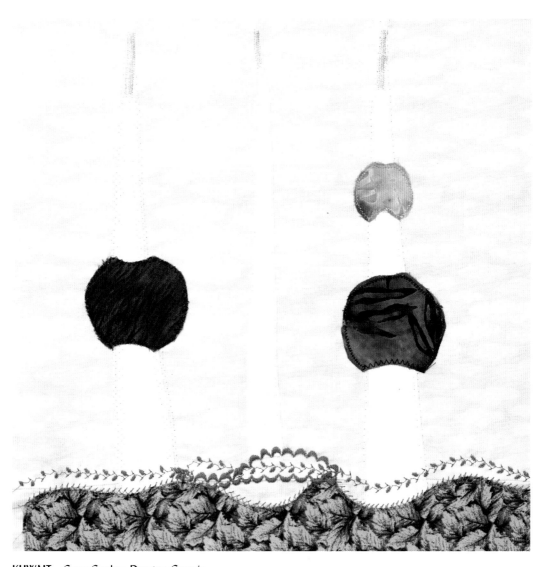

KUWAIT—Gwen Gordon, Decatur, Georgia

"The Kuwait Towers are among the most recognizable landmarks in all of Kuwait. Built in 1975, the tallest tower contains a revolving restaurant, cafeteria, and observation deck. The middle tower serves as a water reservoir and the more spike-like and smallest tower helps to illuminate the other two."

KYRGYZSTAN—designed by Meredith Burdulis*, Dacula, Georgia; made by Holly Anderson*, Cumming, Georgia

"Inspiration for this block came from some photos of the Kyrgyzstan countryside. The purple mountains rise behind green meadows filled with yellow wildflowers. The combination of colors, set against a clear blue daytime sky, is breathtaking!"

Lebanon

LEBANON—Marianne Burrows, Lawrenceville, Georgia

"Embroidered here in the heart of the block, against a background of mountains and a river, the cedar is one of the most cherished symbols of Lebanon. Traditional star blocks, joined by a triple border in the colors of the Lebanese flag, frame the central motif. Many ancient civilizations used the wood of the cedar in religious ceremonies and to build ships, houses, and temples, its resin in mummification, and its bark for circumcision and for the treatment of leprosy. Only small remnants of the ancient forests remain, but extensive reforestation is ongoing."

Maldives

MALDIVES—Elizabeth Barton*, Athens, Georgia

"The block portrays a date palm, which grows in these islands. It incorporates portions of the flag and the national arms. I tried to give a sense of the bright light I imagine in those faraway islands and the constant presence of the ocean horizon."

Mongolia

MONGOLIA—Michele Bautsch, Marietta, Georgia

"The colors I used are from the Mongolian flag. Horses galloping across the steppes were the first thing I thought of when I saw the word Mongolia!"

Nepal

NEPAL—Patsy Eckman*, Cumming, Georgia

"Nepal is a tiny country nestled within the Himalayan mountains. The traditional 'Delectable Mountains' block portrayed in the colors of the Nepalese flag seemed eminently suitable to me to depict a country known for its extraordinary mountains."

Oman

OMAN—Helen Thompson, Avondale Estates, Georgia

Hamsa/Healing Hand/Hand of Fatima

"Hamsa is an ancient symbol of protection used by many cultures. It is called the Hand of Fatima by Muslims, the hamsa hand in Arabic, and hamesh hand in Hebrew. This symbol predates Judaism and Islam and refers to an ancient Middle Eastern Goddess whose hand wards off the Evil Eye. The Hamsa's protective energy is said to attract good luck, happiness, riches, and good health. There is usually an image in the center of the hand: eye, spiral, and heart designs are common."

PAKISTAN—Kathy Oppelt, Lawrenceville, Georgia

"I chose to focus on the peaceful side of a country that has suffered its share of war and strife. Inspiration for this landscape block was taken from Pakistan's spectacular mountains and rivers."

Palestine

PALESTINE—Belinda Pedroso, Atlanta, Georgia

My Three Wise Men

"In this piece I have an opportunity to share symbols of my faith. These symbols, I believe, are universal and can lead to mending bridges between cultures and people. My inspiration for this block is the Dome of the Rock."

Qatar

QATAR—Design by Lindsay Moss*, Roswell, Georgia. Made by Beverly Simpson*, Norcross, Georgia

"The unusual sawtooth pattern in the Qatari flag and its distinctive burgundy color inspired this block. Although a traditional nine-patch, it does not seem so due to the colors and the placement of the many triangles and diamonds, which form the design. Combining several of these blocks results in interesting secondary designs."

Russia

RUSSIA—Jul Kamen*, Georgetown, Texas

Baba Yaga's House on Chicken Legs

According to the Russian fairy tale, Baba Yaga is an old hag who lives deep in the woods in a house on chicken legs. Children who venture too far from home risk being caught by her, thrown in the oven, and eaten! Our parents and grandparents used these old world tales to scare the living daylights out of us, which effectively kept us safe. The 'house on chicken legs' is actually a traditional method of raised construction in Eastern Europe intended to keep food supplies safe from animals. Houses and storage sheds are built upon the tall stumps of closely growing trees, with the roots resembling chicken feet."

SAUDI ARABIA—Jamie Brown, Tampa, Florida

"I feel so honored to be a part of this country block project! The kingdom of Saudi Arabia offers a unique and spectacular landscape. I chose to incorporate the camel in this block, based on my vision of riding across the desert sands. The block is a combination of appliqué and embroidery work."

Sri Lanka

SRI LANKA—Sandy Henry*, Dahlonega, Georgia

"Sri Lanka's strategic location along trade and sea routes in the Indian Ocean makes it a bustling locale for commerce. Among its principal exports are cinnamon, coconuts, and Ceylon tea. I chose the crazy patchwork style to symbolize both the diversity of the people and the diversity of its trade. I used the colors of its flag to honor the country, its long, 3000+ year history, and its people."

Syria

SYRIA—Holly Anderson*, Cumming, Georgia

"Syria is known for its production of beautiful ceramic tiles that adorn everything from doorways to kitchens to places of worship. Often, tiles depicting a connecting vine create an attractive border decoration. The tiles depict a wide variety of motifs, some of which are featured in this fanciful vase."

Tajikistan

TAJIKISTAN—Linda Christensen, Atlanta, Georgia

"I selected the mid-Asian ibex to represent Tajikistan because it is a symbol of the wild mountains that cover so much of the country. Even though there are high mountains, the views are also of tremendous space and brilliant sky. The ibex is placed low in the block so there is more blue behind it, representing that sky. The 'flying geese' at the right go from wildflowers at the bottom up through the green of grasslands and then darker hills, rising finally into the sky."

Turkey

TURKEY—Sharon Henderson*, Lilburn, Georgia

"This block is an interpretation of a picture I saw in an old *National Geographic* magazine I was perusing while sitting in a doctor's waiting room! I was struck by the contrast of the vivid orange sky against the silhouettes of the ancient and exotic architecture. Once I found the fabric, the design simply came forth. Having made this block, I am now drawn to all things Turkish! I would love to travel there someday."

Turkmenistan

TURKMENISTAN—Diane Estrumse Taylor*, Kennesaw, Georgia

"Color contrast is important in this design. I used bright green, maroon, and white because these are the main colors of the flag of Turkmenistan. The texture on the print of the white fabric looks like a parched and cracked desert— about 70% of Turkmenistan is desert. Most of the people are of the Muslim faith, thus I chose a tile pattern design common in Islamic architecture and decorative art. This is a tessellating pattern and is meant to be repeated to the left, right, above, and below."

United Arab Emirates

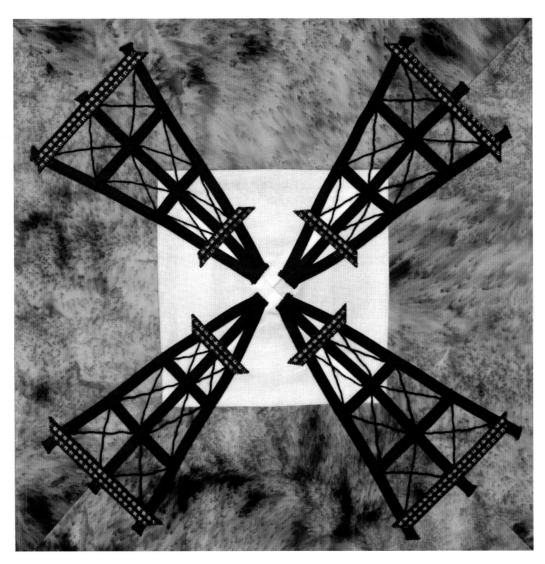

UNITED ARAB EMIRATES—Betty Duff, Milford, Michigan

"The United Arab Emirates is known, among other things, for its production of oil. The bright blue batik background fabric represents the sparkling blue waters of the Persian Gulf that borders the country on one side."

Uzbekistan

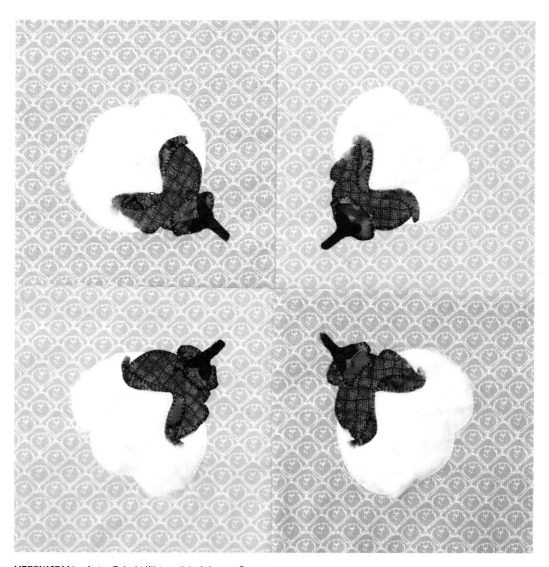

UZBEKISTAN—Anita Zaleski Weinraub*, Atlanta, Georgia

"As soon as I learned that Uzbekistan was one of the world's foremost exporters of cotton, I knew that would be the theme for my block. The background hints at the colors of the country's flag, and I decided to use some raw Georgia cotton to add some dimensionality. After the United States, and depending on the year, Uzbekistan is the world's second, third or fourth largest exporter of cotton."

Yemen

YEMEN—Holly Anderson*, Cumming, Georgia

"I thought it would be fun to work with 'negative space' when making this block. Several people have asked me what language I used and what it said on the bottom sill of the attic window—it's simply the name of the country! I used a vase of flowers to express the joy and security of peace on a cloudless day. The black and white stripes of the vase represent the strife of the past and the hope for the future."

SOUTHEAST ASIA, OCEANIA AND WESTERN PACIFIC RIM

SOUTHEAST ASIA, OCEANIA, AND WESTERN PACIFIC RIM BALLOON—Ben Hollingsworth, Alpharetta, Georgia

"The dragon is used throughout most east Asian cultures as a symbol of incredible strength, imperial authority, and power over nature. The image wrapped around the balloon is made with individual scales, which were painted on fabric, cut out, and applied to a stabilizer. The face has an eye made from polymer paint and embroidery stitches."

Fabrics chosen for the balloon represent fabric designs that use symbols of western Pacific Rim cultures. I also used graphic designs associated with Indonesia, Japan, China, Australia, Hawaii, and others.

This balloon was created with paper piecing. If you're a quilter, you know that this technique can be tedious and frustrating. However, it was the only way to achieve the precision needed to realize my vision, so I stuck with it (even if I made four strips backwards and had to re-sew several seams as many as ten times to get it right)!"

American Samoa

AMERICAN SAMOA—Ben Hollingsworth, Alpharetta, Georgia

"Using Polynesian Batik fabrics, I created an image that represents the most common icons of life in American Samoa: A dancer, a ukulele-playing musician, and a grass-roofed hut are gathered on the beach with bright blue water and large volcanic mountains in the background. Extensive threadwork helped to achieve the look I was after."

Australia

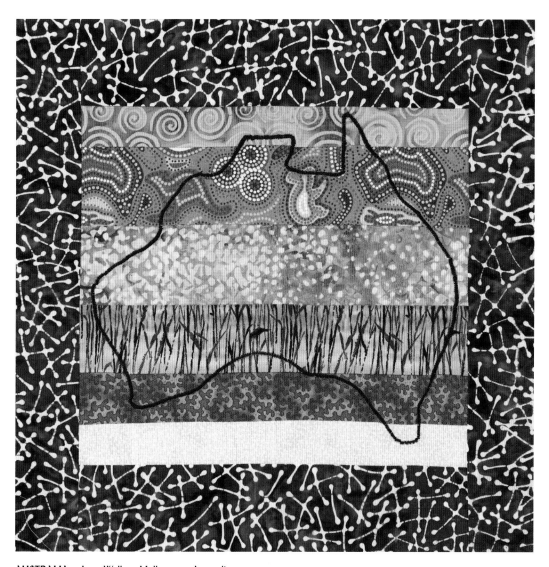

AUSTRALIA—Joan Walker, Melbourne, Australia

Stanza 2 of the Australian national poem, "My Country" by Dorothea McKellar, inspired this block:

I love a sunburnt country,
A land of sweeping plains,
Of ragged mountain ranges,
Of droughts and flooding rains.
I love her far horizons,
I love her jewel-sea,
Her beauty and her terror—
The wide brown land for me!

Brunei Darussalam

BRUNEI DARUSSALAM—Jane Grayson* and Cathy Skrypek*, Cumming, Georgia

"The name of this country, 'Brunei, Abode of Peace' led us to portray these pinwheels, made in the colors of the flag, which we imagine spinning and blowing freely in the breeze. This sultanate, located on the north shore of the island of Borneo, derives about half of its GDP from crude oil and natural gas production, which is represented in the block by the black spikes of the pinwheel pattern."

Cambodia

CAMBODIA—Nancy McCurdy*, Gale Probst*, Margaret Stent*, and Betty Wolfrom*, Stone Mountain, Georgia

"Large green triangles represent the Kravanah Mountains in Southwest Cambodia, framing a rising or setting sun. In this way, we echo the pattern of our 'Mary's Triangles' quilt, which was given to Cambodia during the 1996 Atlanta Olympic Games."

Cook Islands

COOK ISLANDS—Sheila Blair*, Atlanta, Georgia

"Polynesian folklore is replete with tales featuring sea turtles. Vital to regional lifestyle and culture, they are icons of creation and power and are often the subject of traditional tattoos. I deliberately chose fabrics with little contrast in order to give the impression that my turtle is swimming underwater!"

East Timor

EAST TIMOR—Wanda Hickman*, Dunwoody, Georgia

"East Timor is in Southeast Asia at the eastern end of the Indonesian Archipelago. One of the world's newest countries, its people have developed a number of industries to support the economy. Coffee, silver jewelry, and beautiful hand-woven textiles are purchased by tourists and exported as well. This quilt block is dedicated to the industry and beauty of the people of East Timor."

Fiji

FIJI—Clare Gilliland, Rome, Georgia

"This block represents a typical beach on the gorgeous Fiji Islands. The boat is representative of a popular pastime, and the hut reminds the viewer of the nation's indigenous Polynesian roots.

Appliqué is a great way to interpret what we see in nature and incorporate it into our fiber art. It allows us to use colorations not found in nature and create whimsical environments. We are limited only by our imaginations."

Guam

GUAM—Debbie Campbell, Suffolk, Virginia

"The latte stone is an ancient stone pillar found in the Marianas Islands (Guam is part of this archipelago) and it is the unofficial symbol of Guam. The pillars were probably used as building supports. Latte stones show the ingenuity and skill of early dwellers of this beautiful island."

Hong Kong

HONG KONG—Cindy Rounds Richards*, Snellville, Georgia

"When I was nine years old, my family moved to Thailand. We visited Hong Kong on the way, which gave me an immediate vision for my block of a cityscape and a 'junk'. This block was a joy to make."

Indonesia

INDONESIA—Elly Williams, Lilburn, Georgia

"Choosing a subject for my block was simple when I learned how many live volcanoes there are in Indonesia. The beautiful landscapes were also an inspiration and I soon decided to portray them in my own interpretation of Indonesia. The volcano and the smoke are depicted with intricate threadwork."

Japan

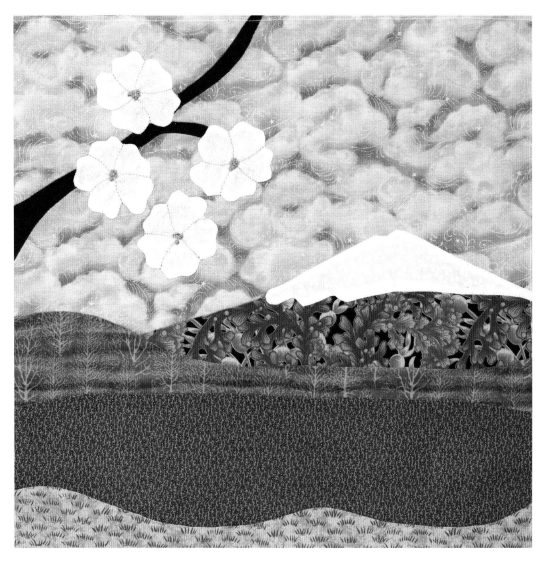

JAPAN—Pat Fielding*, Columbia, Missouri

"When I think of Japan, I think of beautiful flowers, snow-capped mountains, and luscious fields and rivers. The beautiful and gentle landscape of Japan is a reflection of the people and the country. I was very proud that Japan received my Olympic quilt."

Kiribati

KIRIBATI—Cathy Skrypek*, Cumming, Georgia

"The tropical location of this island nation inspired my color choices for this block. I imagined the bright gold of the sun and the reflective shades of blue of the sea and sky that surround the islands. Because Kiribati straddles the equator and is just west of the international date line, it is the first nation to see the dawn of each day!"

North Korea

NORTH KOREA—Nellie Giddens*, Macon, Georgia

"The national flower of North Korea is the Siebold's Magnolia, a hardy, east Asian species. The tree represents strength and its flower beauty. Since the magnolia (albeit a different species) is found throughout my home state of Georgia, I decided to use it in my North Korea block. I used the Georgia Quilt Project's magnolia pattern to create my appliquéd block."

South Korea

SOUTH KOREA—Shirley Erickson*, Athens, Georgia

"My fan creates a light breeze that blows across the beautiful fields surrounding the honorable and gentle people who work and live in this beautiful country. Fans are a symbol of a rich tradition and culture and their design and use are considered an art form in Korea."

Laos

LAOS—Mary Lou Mojonnier*, Atlanta, Georgia

"This block is in the colors of the Laotian flag—red bands on top and bottom, blue band in center, and white in the middle. I chose the square within a square motif, inspired by some Laotian (Hmong) needlework that I own."

Malaysia

MALAYSIA—Maru Mattimoe, Atlanta, Georgia

"Petronas Towers in Kuala Lumpur, a skyscraper of eighty-eight floors, comprises the top portion of my block. It represents growth and technology. Unfortunately, this development is frequently in conflict with the natural beauty and the rainforests, depicted at the bottom of the block by photo transfers of, from left, the silver leaf monkey, the orangutan, and the capuchin monkey." *Photos by Michael Fountain.*

Marshall Islands

MARSHALL ISLANDS—Amanda Langford, San Antonio, Florida

"To convey the essence of the Marshall Islands, an island nation in the Pacific, I chose to mimic the simple design of a scuba dive flag, as the Islands offer world class scuba diving. As part of the culture, exceptional navigational skills have been passed down through the generations, hence the fabric selection of blue, which also symbolizes the ocean. The orange and white denote the two major island chains while also representing peace and courage. The embroidered star in the center represents the cross of Christianity, which is important to the culture of the Islands and which has twenty-four points, one for each district, while the four elongated points represent principal cultural centers."

Micronesia

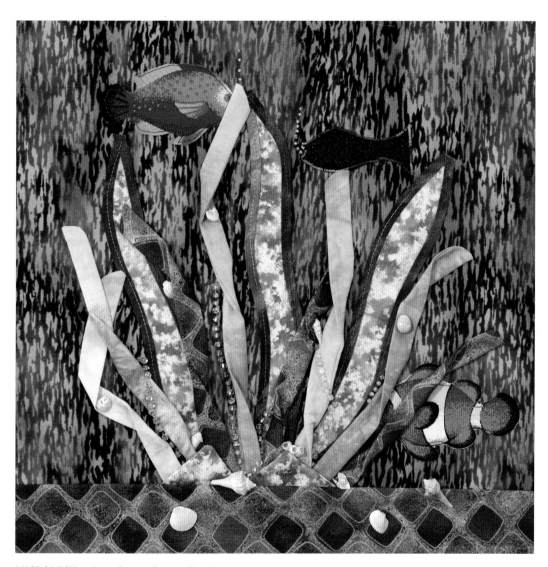

MICRONESIA—Jamie Brown, Tampa, Florida

"This block reflects the beautiful seas and the coral reefs found on many islands in the South Pacific. I used batiks that were the colors of the sea. The coral is three-dimensional, tacked down with sea shells I found on the beach near my home. The fish are a combination of embroidery work and appliqué. This is my vision of the beautiful country of Micronesia."

Myanmar (Burma)

MYANMAR (BURMA)—Linda Bitley*, Marietta, Georgia

"This same block was used in my 'Amazing Georgia' quilt, which was given to Myanmar at the 1996 Atlanta Olympic Games. It is an original design, but is based on the construction techniques used in the traditional 'Log Cabin' pattern. Each block uses only two fabrics, a green pattern and a plain color chosen from among the minor hues in the green fabric. Using a triangle in each color to create the center block permits the strips used to make the rest of the block to appear to wind around each other in a spiral pattern. Each spiral connects to the spiral in the next block, creating an interlocking surface pattern."

Nauru

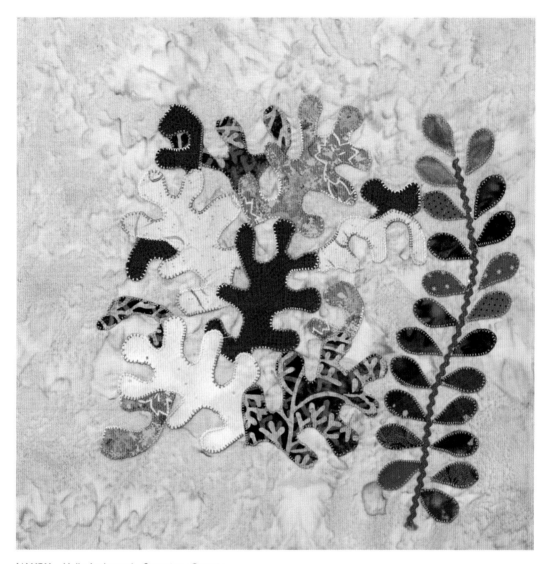

NAURU—Holly Anderson*, Cumming, Georgia

"Sometimes the beauty of a country is not readily apparent. Nauru is a rock island in the South Pacific whose extensive phosphate reserves have been virtually exhausted. However, the island is surrounded by beautiful coral reefs, which are exposed at low tide. These coral formations are home to many finfish, and provide a beautiful array of pink, peach, and yellow coral."

New Zealand

NEW ZEALAND—Mary Ruth McDonald, Roswell, Georgia

"New Zealand's unique native flora and fauna provided inspiration for this block. The Kiwi bird has long been adapted as representing New Zealanders, aka 'Kiwis', and the Silver Fern tree, which grows up to ten meters high, is widely used as a symbol for New Zealand sports teams. I appliquéd a 'funky' fabric silhouette of a kiwi and a stylized silver fern frond soaring above the kiwi on a busy olive green background. These two motifs signify, to me, 'New Zealandness'."

Palau

PALAU—Danese Ballantine, Lawrenceville, Georgia

"Palau is an island nation in the South Pacific. It is tropical with beaches, palm trees, and rock islands, and of course it is surrounded by the beautiful blue ocean."

Papua New Guinea

PAPUA NEW GUINEA—Annette Desautels*, Acworth, Georgia

"Papua New Guinea's flag colors are red, black, yellow, and white—the outer perimeter of the block reflects this. The island of Papua New Guinea has snow-capped mountains, exotic birds of paradise, rain forests, and beaches. Each of these is depicted in a separate quadrant of the block."

Philippines

PHILIPPINES—Cody Anne Moss, Alpharetta, Georgia

"What better way to represent the vibrancy of a nation's culture than portraying its national dance? Tinikling is the most popular and best known of Philippine folk dances. My portrait is of dancers 'tinikling', skillfully jumping between bamboo poles as they imitate the movements of the native Tikling birds from which the dance derives its name. The 1-2-3 rhythm is pleasant and lively. Tinikling dancing is not only artistic but athletic as well."

Singapore

SINGAPORE—Molly Samuels, Norcross, Georgia

"My block depicts the famous Merlion statue, which overlooks Marina Bay in Singapore. The merlion, a mythical creature with the body of a fish and the head of a lion, serves as the symbol of Singapore. 'Mer', meaning 'sea', is a nod to Singapore's origins as a fishing village. The lion's head symbolizes Singapore's original name—Singapura—which means lion city. Extensive machine threadwork emphasizes details on the statue."

Solomon Islands

SOLOMON ISLANDS—Jane Barwick, Rome, Georgia

"The archipelago of the Solomon Islands is truly a tropical paradise. Pristine white beaches, rainforest jungle, and crystalline ocean are just part of the wonders to be found there! I tried to represent these in my block, and I included a primitive longboat, a reminder of the people of these islands. Of Polynesian descent, they colonized the islands thousands of years ago, and boats and maritime transportation continue to be integral parts of life on the Solomon Islands today."

Taiwan

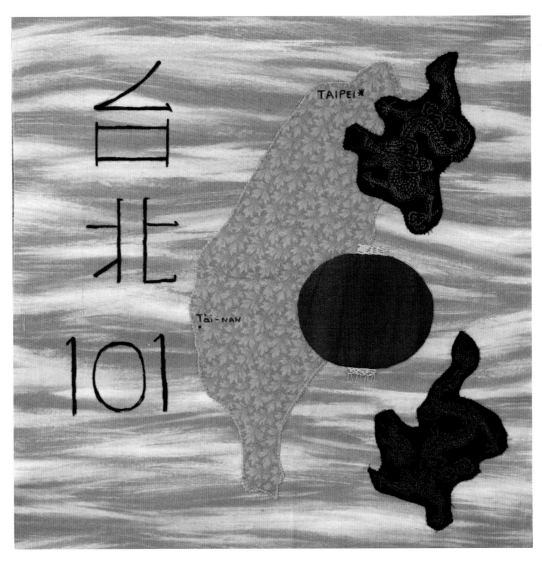

TAIWAN—Cathy MacDonald, Norcross, Georgia

"The Chinese characters spell 'Taipei 101', which is a building in Taipei of which the citizens are very proud. It is symbolic of Taiwan's growth and productivity. My neighbor from Taiwan suggested this and wrote the characters for me."

Thailand

THAILAND—Irene McLaren*, Miami, Florida

Thai Beauty

"Thai architecture is characterized by sharply angled temple roofs and many tall, thin spires, with curves and arches at doors and windows. Decorative arts are ornate, with flowers, filigree, and carvings. A land of great visual beauty."

Tonga

TONGA—Elisa Woods, Atlanta, Georgia

"This block represents one side of Tonga's one cent coin, featuring corn, which represents a native crop and productivity. The Kingdom of Tonga is an archipelago in the South Pacific, located about one third of the way between New Zealand and Hawaii. Tonga was also known as the Friendly Islands. The red base block reflects one of the colors of the country's flag."

Tuvalu

TUVALU—Nancy Sohl*, Cumming, Georgia

Tuvalu's coat of arms provided the inspiration for this block. The undulating gold lines against the dark blue background bring to mind waves cresting on the shores of this South Pacific island nation. The nine stars on the Tuvaluan flag, which represent the nine islands comprising Tuvalu, are here reduced to two—neither one pointing upward, consistent with the star placement on the country's flag.

Vanuatu

VANUATU—Sandy Henry*, Dahlonega, Georgia

"A South Pacific volcanic island nation, Vanuatu's economy depends on financial services, cattle herding, and tourism. Recently, tourism has seen a welcomed burst of popularity as many people were introduced to the country through the airing of the US television reality show, 'Survivor: Vanuatu—Islands of Fire.' The eighty-two islands comprising Vanuatu have more than 800 miles of shoreline, providing ample opportunity for visitors who want to 'get away from it all' to do exactly that!'"

Vietnam

VIETNAM—Ben Hollingsworth, Alpharetta, Georgia

"Workers dressed in sedge hats are harvesting rice in the paddies terraced along the hills beside the Mekong River. A wooden boat makes its way upriver to bring another load of rice to the market."

Western Samoa

WESTERN SAMOA—Holly Anderson*, Cumming, Georgia

"Among the textiles indigenous to Western Samoa is 'siapo' or bark cloth. It is made by beating the bark of the mulberry tree until it is soft and pliable. Everyday use of siapo has declined in recent times, but it is still used in ceremonial textiles and costumes."

EUROPE

EUROPE BALLOON—Deborah Steinmann*, Atlanta, Georgia

"The Europe balloon combines the colors and symbols of many European countries. In the background are the mountains, whether the Alps or the Pyrenees, the Apennines or the Carpathians, and nestled in them are Bavaria's Neuschwanstein castle and Luxembourg's castle Vianden. Above all floats a Greek key pattern, and in front of them are three matryoshka dolls, representing several eastern European countries. The first is decorated with a motif borrowed from the Czech Republic block, the second with France's Eiffel Tower, and the third with a painter's palette, representing the rich artistic heritage of Italy.

In making this block, I borrowed motifs from several of the European country blocks, which were very well done and therefore inspiring to work with."

Albania

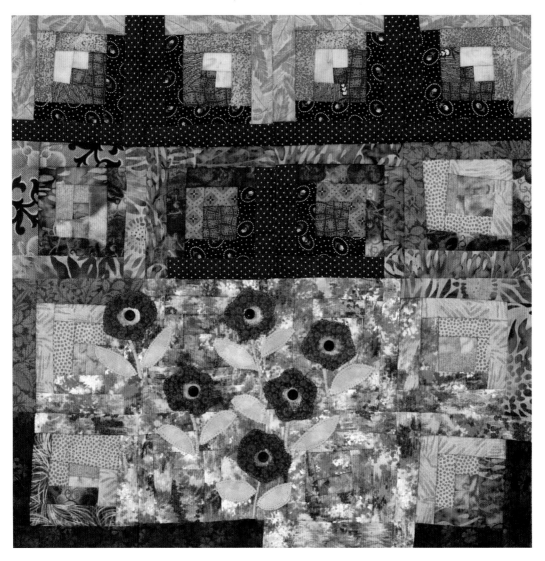

ALBANIA—Holly Anderson*, Cumming, Georgia

"Three inch log cabin blocks form the landscape of my block, representing Albania's mountainous terrain and rich flora and fauna. The country's hills are dotted with patches of wildflowers, including the red and black poppy, which is Albania's national flower. Poppies are raised here both for their medicinal applications and their seeds."

Andorra

ANDORRA—Sandy Henry*, Dahlonega, Georgia

"Against a background of a traditional star block rendered in the colorful hues of the Andorran flag, silhouetted skiers glide down mountainous slopes. The average elevation of Andorra is well over a mile, providing an excellent wintry getaway for tourists. The Andorran air is clear with low humidity and more than 300 days of sunshine per year, making this country a popular tourist mecca in all seasons, not just in winter."

Austria

AUSTRIA—Wanda Hickman*, Dunwoody, Georgia

"This block speaks to the flower-covered and steep mountains of Austria, which are a trademark of the country's natural beauty. The black and white stripes hint at piano keys and symbolize the important place Austria holds in the world of classical music."

Belarus

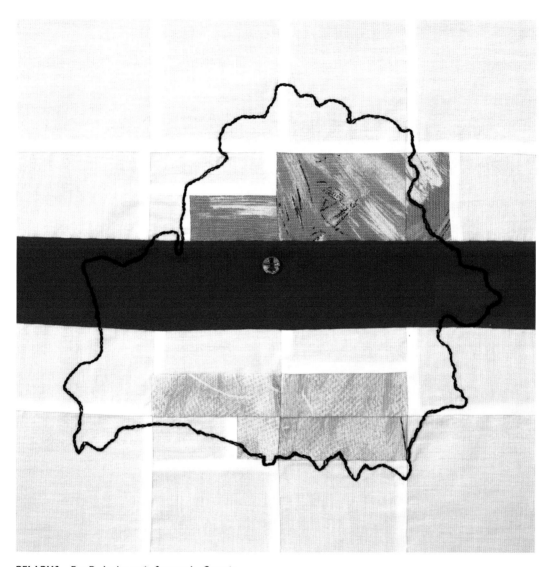

BELARUS—Fay B. Anderson*, Savannah, Georgia

"The flag of Belarus is white with a red central stripe, hence my choice of colors. There are marshes in the south, which are depicted in gold, and trees in the north, reflected in my choice of green fabric. A chain stitch outlines this land-locked country, which is surrounded by Poland, Ukraine, Russia, Latvia, and Lithuania. The 'jewel' button indicates Minsk, the capital and pride of Belarus!"

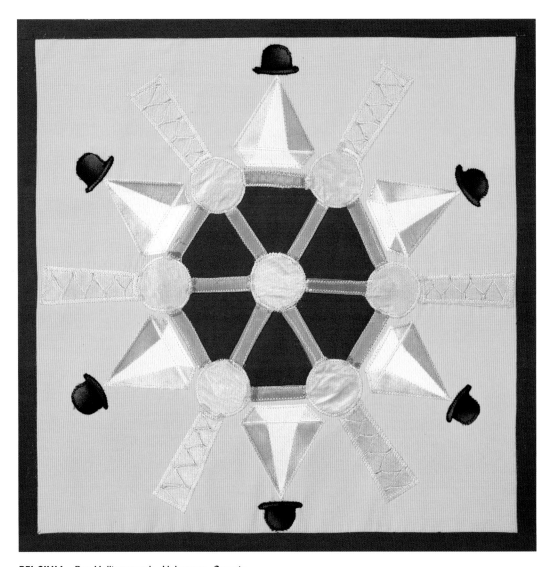

BELGIUM—Ben Hollingsworth, Alpharetta, Georgia

"In this block the Atomium, erected for the 1958 World's Fair in Brussels, is the central radial design element with the stairways appearing as windmills. This hexagonal shape is surrounded by diamonds representing Antwerp, and the derby hats are a nod to one of my favorite artists, René Magritte."

Bosnia and Herzegovina

BOSNIA AND HERZEGOVINA—Jan Antranikian, Alpharetta, Georgia

"I saw a photograph of the beautiful Stari Most (Old Bridge), which is located in Mostar, the largest city of Herzegovina. The bridge was built in the 1400s and is one of the country's most recognizable landmarks. After standing for 423 years, the bridge was destroyed in 1993 during the Croat-Bosniak war. It was rebuilt and reopened in 2004."

Bulgaria

BULGARIA—Holly Anderson*, Cumming, Georgia

"Popular throughout Eastern Europe, the colored eggs or 'pisano yaytse' as they are called in Bulgaria, are a symbol of spring and rebirth. Eggs are presented to family members and close friends as a wish for good health and prosperity. Traditionally the designs were created using a wax resist technique, although today many methods are used."

Croatia

CROATIA—Sue Hunston, Seneca, South Carolina, and Holly Anderson*, Cumming, Georgia

"Inspiration for this block came from Croatia's national sport—soccer. Using the red and white checkerboard with the blue and white border is a nod to the Croatian flag. When four blocks are repeated and set together, a secondary design is formed, making this block quite versatile."

Cyprus

CYPRUS—Kathryn Duggleby, Marietta, Georgia

"A small island nation located in the Mediterranean Sea, Cyprus, in my vision, is a spray of white mountains surrounded by the sea. I used various blues and jewel tones to represent this 'jewel' of the Mediterranean; the white triangles represent the mountains, which are white with snow in winter."

Czech Republic

CZECH REPUBLIC—Deborah Jones, Atlanta, Georgia

"This appliquéd motif was inspired by a hand-painted plate made in the Czech Republic.
It is typical of the kind of traditional floral designs found in Czech folk art."

Denmark

DENMARK—Patty Murphy, Atlanta, Georgia

"The fairy tales of Hans Christian Anderson are beloved by children worldwide. I loved the story of the Little Mermaid when I was a little girl and remember reading it to my grandmother. The mermaid evokes a lot of happy memories. I hope I will be able to pass my love of the story on to my children."

ESTONIA—Meg Latimer, Alpharetta, Georgia

In this block, an oak tree spreads its leaves against a background of the traditional rail fence pattern executed in the colors of the Estonian flag. The oak, long regarded as a sacred tree, is the unofficial symbol of Estonia, denoting strength and resilience. Oak branches appear on the national shield. The colors of Estonia's flag have been described as symbolizing many things, most commonly as follows: the blue represents ancient freedom, as well as the sky. Black is the color of the rich native soil or the black worries of the past. White represents the white sails of ships and a bright future."

Finland

FINLAND—Ginger Haas White*, Marietta, Georgia

"My 'trademark' is incorporating some of my hand painted fabric into whatever I create—you can see it here in the midnight sun. I like taking something traditional and then making it my own. In this block, I simplified the lines of nature in winter to their most minimal forms."

France

FRANCE—Kathy Rennell Forbes*, formerly of Alpharetta, Georgia

The iconic landmark depicted in this block makes one want to burst into song… 'Allons enfants de la patrie…!' In this interpretation, this most recognized structure of Paris is pieced in horizontal strips; embroidered embellishments finish the edges of each level. The Eiffel Tower was erected for the 1889 *Exposition Universelle* in Paris and was originally painted red. At the time, it was the tallest man-made structure in the world and remained so until the Chrysler Building was built in New York City in 1930. Controversial and deemed "ugly" and "grotesque" by many critics (including de Maupassant, Zola, and Dumas the Younger) at the time it was built, 'la tour Eiffel' is now a beloved landmark and source of pride for the French people.

Germany

GERMANY—Deborah Steinmann*, Atlanta, Georgia

"My husband Matt is German and collects steins, so this became the inspiration for my block. My stein is central and anchors the other elements—the mountains, including Neuschwanstein Castle, the Black Forest, and beer! The Beatles spent much of their early days singing at clubs in Hamburg."

GREECE—Design by Barbara Sanders*, formerly of Watkinsville, Georgia. Made by Holly Anderson*, Cumming, Georgia

"What could be more iconically Greek than the Parthenon, the ancient temple of Athena? Set atop the Acropolis, it was a symbol of Greece's political and cultural sophistication hundreds of years before Cicero or Caesar were even born. I have superimposed this image of the Parthenon over blue and white, colors of the Greek flag. These colors also represent the white, sun bleached land of Greece, and the blue ocean along which the country traces an extensive coastline. A Greek key pattern in the outer border completes the block."

Hungary

HUNGARY—Gay Hollinger, Stone Mountain, Georgia

"My block depicts the Parliament Building in Budapest as seen from across the Danube River. My own photos inspired this block. I loved the spires and wonderful architecture. The setting by the river was beautiful."

Iceland

ICELAND—Lisa Throneberry, Murfreesboro, Tennessee

"Iceland is a country of ice and snow and cold temperatures sitting on top of volcanic heat and turmoil. The clean air, the lush mountains, and the volcanic landscape fascinate and entrance all who set foot on this charmed land. This block uses die-cut, fused shapes."

Ireland

IRELAND—Kathy O'Meara Magnuson, Lawrenceville, Georgia

"Ireland: The Emerald Isle and thirty-nine other shades of green—a common perception. While the color green abounds, there's so much more to the Irish landscape; it's the latter that I wished to depict in my block representing this country.

I chose images I believe to be compelling in their stark beauty, with origins in the far past, graphic simplicity in the present, with echoes likely to be far-reaching into the future. Straightforward, effective photographs: a high cross from Clonmacnoise (a monastic site overlooking the River Shannon in County Offaly) and a cathedral wall on the site of St. Declan's monastery in Ardmore, County Waterford; it is believed to be the oldest Christian settlement in Ireland.

I chose the Kaleidoscope block not only for its aesthetic appeal, but also because it represents 360 degrees—all of life comes full circle." (*Original photographs by the Artist*)

Italy

ITALY—Kathy McGill, Beaufort, South Carolina

"This block is a celebration of the many industries and talents of the Italian people. Represented in machine embroidery are movies, art, fashion, Roman architecture, music, the cuisine, wineries, and olive oil production, with a map of the country in the center."

Kosovo

KOSOVO—Alice Berg*, Atlanta, Georgia

"My quilting journey goes back many years; it began with simple patchwork, which is still a favorite of mine today. Sewing squares and triangles of different fabrics together, then watching them form a design never grows old. I often include houses, pretending to live in each one! In my block, the different fabrics also represent the diverse ethnicities of the people of Kosovo that, despite their physical, cultural, and linguistic differences, nevertheless come together to form a cohesive nation."

Latvia

LATVIA—Livija Marta Rieksts Bolster, Atlanta, Georgia

"I chose to depict Latvia by using a variation of the star symbol found in its ancient and contemporary folk art. I put the design on a background of trees—birch trees that are native to Latvia and that my mother often spoke of with great fondness. Latvia is a low-lying country with rich loam deposits cut by numerous streams and rivers flowing to the Baltic Sea—represented by the blue cloth. Latvia's many castles are represented by the yellow sun-star fabric in the middle of the block. The exterior X's or crosses are another symbol found in Latvian decorative art, and also allude to the thick forests."

Liechtenstein

LIECHTENSTEIN—Julie Monroe, Gainesville, Georgia

"My block is based on a picture of Vaduz Castle in the tiny Grand Duchy of Liechtenstein. I deconstructed the castle into three separate dwellings and then used paper piecing to construct them. I surrounded them with the mountains and forests which comprise this precious land."

Lithuania

LITHUANIA—Priscilla Ordway, Roswell, Georgia

"Lithuania is an amazing country. It was hard to choose what to highlight in my block, but when I learned that its literacy rate is 99.6%, I decided to make a book block. The Lithuanian flag is yellow, green, and red—hence my color choices."

Luxembourg

LUXEMBOURG—Cody Ann Moss, Alpharetta, Georgia

"Classic European fairy tale castles come to mind when I think of Luxembourg, so I just knew I had to depict one of the country's famous castles. Castle Vianden has stood since Roman times as a symbol of Luxembourg's strength and importance as a center point of the European continent."

Macedonia

MACEDONIA—Akiko Matsumoto, Atlanta, Georgia

"I have named this block 'Fifty Lakes and Sixteen Mountains', because it is said that there are fifty lakes and sixteen mountains in Macedonia, among other things. Many people visit to see this beautiful landscape mosaic. So, I designed the geometrical lines for the block, as if the images are transforming from concrete to abstract. I would love to see those beautiful lakes in person and take a deep breath."

MALTA – Candi Reed, Douglas, Georgia

"The Maltese Cross was an obvious choice for my block. The bright blue, yellow, and red strips are the traditional colors of the Malta fishing boats with the blue starting at the water line. Malta is a Mediterranean island nation known for its seafaring tradition."

MOLDOVA—Beth Culp*, Atlanta, Georgia

"Traditional Moldovan pottery was the design inspiration for my block. The shape of the pot is similar to those produced by Moldovan artists and I have embellished the braid around the pot with French knots of perle cotton to replicate the texture of the pottery. I was drawn to making a block for this country because my daughter Erin served in the Peace Corps there."

Monaco

MONACO—Gay Hollinger, Stone Mountain, Georgia

Casino Monte Carlo

"I chose to represent the iconic Monte Carlo Casino in my block, a beautiful building whose architecture makes me think of a palace. I also wanted to contrast the polished sophistication of the building with the natural beauty of this tiny country, complete with soaring birds and exotic plant life, which make this nation a paradise both culturally and naturally. My photos and the memory of a great vacation inspired this block."

Montenegro

MONTENEGRO – Shirley McKenzie*, Jackson, Georgia

"Montenegro, which means 'black mountain', has one of the most rugged mountain terrains in Europe. It is also home to one of the few remaining European rain forests and the second-longest canyon in the world. More than one million tourists visit Montenegro annually, primarily to enjoy its beautiful beaches along the Adriatic Sea. My block attempts to highlight all these aspects of Montenegro—the vast forests are represented by the tree. The four-patches set on point represent the blue sky and sea, the beaches, and the red of the national flag."

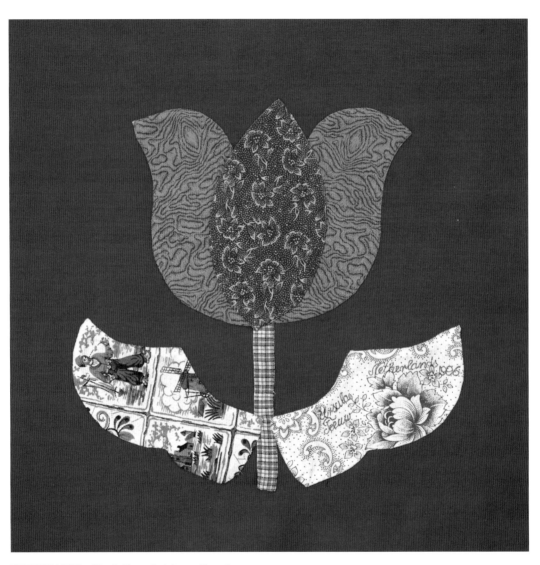

NETHERLANDS—Ursula Teeuw*, Atlanta, Georgia

"I made this block with my Dutch background in mind. Also called Holland, the Netherlands is famous for its canals and waterworks. Wooden shoes and tulips are also well known aspects of Dutch culture and landscape. The blue background of my block represents the water and the tulip and its clog 'leaves' complete the picture. The stem of the tulip and the clogs are made of Dutch fabrics, which are used for making our national dress."

Norway

NORWAY—Dorothy Kenney*, Stone Mountain, Georgia

"Historically a seafaring people, Norwegians are proud of their maritime heritage. This is what I chose to portray in my block. A stylized single-masted Viking ship, set against a blue sky, plies the northern waters in search of ... new discoveries perhaps?"

Poland

POLAND—Anita Zaleski Weinraub*, Atlanta, Georgia

"Historically, Poland has often been caught between nations in its centuries-old struggle for independence, and I have tried to reflect this in my block. Depicted here in a crazy-patch style block, today's Poland is surrounded by seven nations. Beginning at the Baltic Sea and going clockwise, they are: Russia, Lithuania, Belarus, Ukraine, Slovakia, Czech Republic and Germany. The 'syrenka', or mermaid, is the symbol of Warsaw, the capital of Poland. Embroidered trees and stacks of wheat represent Poland's extensive forests and abundant farmlands. Embroidery embellishes the borders between nations, consistent with the crazy-patch style. This design was inspired by my dear friend, Maria Grochowska of Skarzisko-Kamienne, Poland."

Portugal

PORTUGAL—Holly Anderson*, Cumming, Georgia

"This folk art style rooster or 'galo de Barcelos' has become the unofficial symbol of Portugal. It is often featured in ceramic designs as well as in embroidered textiles and in a variety of tourist trinkets. It is said to bring the owner good luck."

ROMANIA—Meg Fisher*, Marietta, Georgia

"I have always liked the traditional Attic Windows pattern—it is so versatile! In my interpretation, the fractured diagonal striped block is nicely framed with this pattern. I thought it was more pleasing to the eye to make four framed blocks rather than just one large one. The colors pay tribute to the flag of Romania."

San Marino

SAN MARINO—Lauren Finley, Powder Springs, Georgia

"The Republic of San Marino is the oldest surviving sovereign state and constitutional republic in the world—it was established in 301 A.D. as a monastic community. Its current constitution has been in effect since 1600. This raw-edged appliqué block represents Guaita, one of three towers situated on mountain peaks in the capital city. Guaita is the oldest tower, built in the eleventh century."

SERBIA—Holly Anderson*, Cumming, Georgia

"Serbia has a strong tradition of woven textiles, which represent the Serbian people and their culture. Each cloth or rug is not only a decorative design, but a symbol of the passing down of a tradition to the present generation."

Slovakia

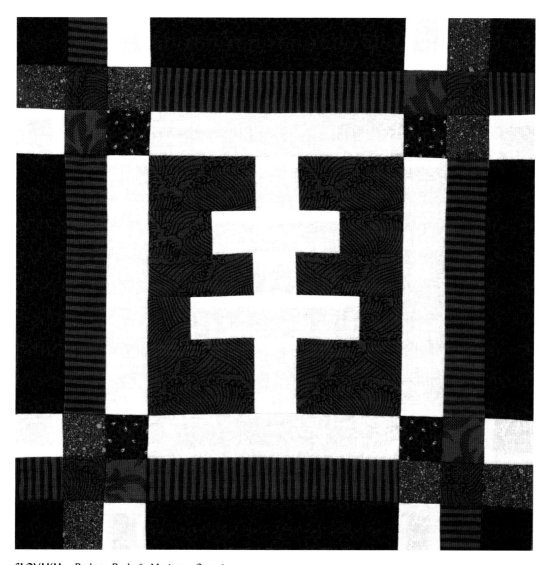

SLOVAKIA—Barbara Butler*, Marietta, Georgia

"The block design is based on the Slovakian flag. The color of stripes is in the order of white, blue, and red as they appear on the flag. The center block is based on the design used on a red shield, which appears in the center of the flag. Nine-patch blocks and rails surround the symbol in my block."

Slovenia

SLOVENIA—Lauren Rose*, Lilburn, Georgia

"The Church of the Assumption seems to float above the water, due to its location on a small island on Lake Bled. It is a Slovenian tradition for newlyweds to row to the island and for the groom to carry his bride up the ninety-nine steep steps to the top! I used a fusible applique technique and embroidery stitches to create the surrounding bushes."

Spain

SPAIN—Nicole Blackwell, Ellenwood, Georgia

"Bullfighting is a longstanding tradition in Spain. This form of celebration mixes skill and artistry with courage and luck to mesmerize an expectant audience. Dressed in his finest 'traje de luces (suit of lights)', this block depicts the elegant dance between man and beast—the Matador and the bull."

Sweden

SWEDEN—Deborah Jones, Sandy Springs, Georgia

"The dala horse has long been an unofficial symbol of Sweden, and these wooden horses, in all sizes and usually painted a vibrant red/orange, are ubiquitous throughout the country. My interpretation of this popular souvenir is set against a background of the traditional Starry Path block done in the colors of Sweden's flag, to honor the country's abundance of starry skies and sunny days."

SWITZERLAND—Jan Curran Vincent*, Big Canoe, Georgia

"I've had a fascination with Switzerland since receiving a View-Master slide show of Switzerland for Christmas when I was about ten years old! I was thus delighted when I learned that the quilt I had made for the 1996 Olympic Games would be presented to the Swiss Olympic Committee. I designed this block to capture the majestic Swiss Alps, a friendly cottage with flowering window boxes, and I also including a stylized Swiss flag."

UKRAINE—Debbie Russell*, Decatur, Georgia

"I chose the nesting dolls to represent Ukraine. To me, they were a perfect example of a time-honored handicraft of that country ... just as was my gift of a quilt to the Ukraine during the 1996 Atlanta Olympic Games."

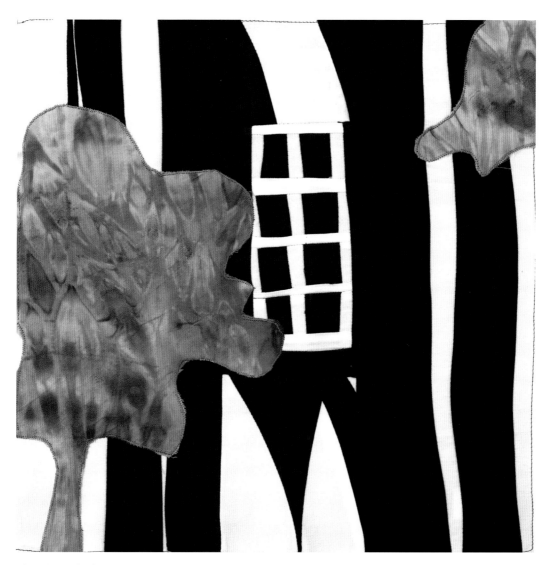

UNITED KINGDOM—Elizabeth Barton*, Athens, Georgia

"This block incorporates things I love most about my home country. I love the remembrances of times long ago that are everywhere; the medieval houses made from beams curving as naturally as did the trees they came from, and ancient walls and roads. There are so many parks full of trees—especially the oak, which portrays steadfastness and traditional British tenacity."

Vatican City

VATICAN CITY—Kathy McGill, Beaufort, South Carolina

"This block takes the viewer on a symbolic tour of some of the treasures of the Vatican. Included are some of the art, architecture, and religious artifacts in this world-renowned home of the Pope and of the Catholic Church. Machine embroidery was used to create the images."

AFRICA

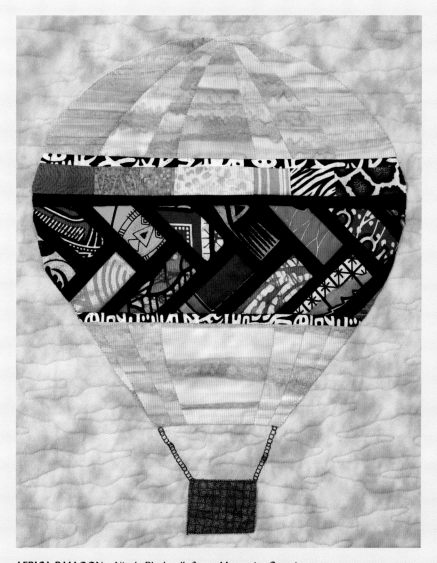

AFRICA BALLOON—Nicole Blackwell, Stone Mountain, Georgia

"To experience Africa is to be immersed in rich cultures, breathtaking landscapes, and abundant wildlife. There is surely no other place like it on Earth. It could be said that this experience has also been woven into the fabrics of the region. Full of color, texture, pattern, and meaning, African fabrics tell a story that is unique to their homeland.

Representing Africa, this hot air balloon brings together many of the elements that define the continent. The orange batik background reflects the warm sun that bathes the region's occupants. Animal fabrics introduce the wild inhabitants one might encounter on an African safari. The central braid design weaves together the varied regional fabrics depicting Africa's people, traditions, and village life. Lastly, the black and white border fabric mimics the popular, hand-dyed West African mud cloth."

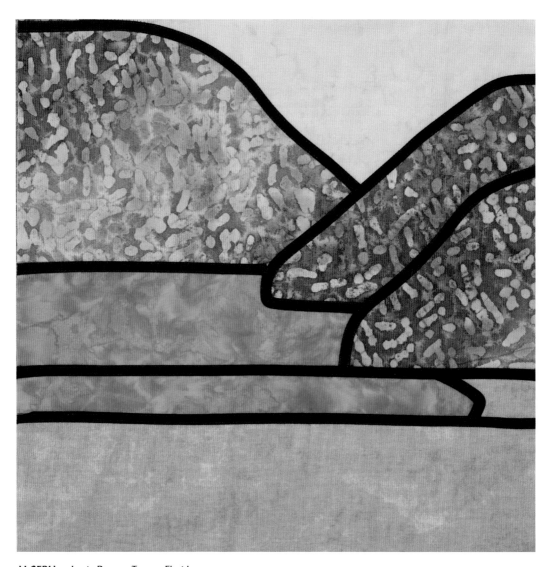

ALGERIA—Jamie Brown, Tampa, Florida

"I find the landscape of Algeria to be spectacularly beautiful. This block incorporates the country's magnificent mountains, the sea, and the desert. The block was designed in the stained glass appliqué style using enriched fabrics to show the beauty of the country."

Angola

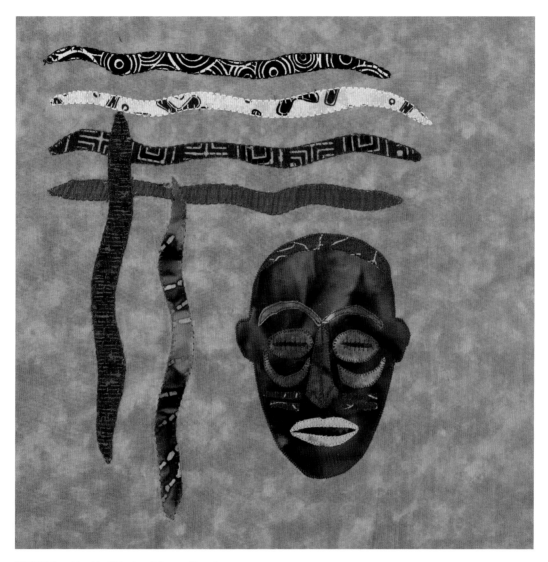

ANGOLA—Aleathia Chisolm, Atlanta, Georgia

"Wooden masks and sculptures are among the most famous symbols in Angolan art. Noted for their aesthetic beauty, these masks play an important role in cultural rituals that celebrate birth and death, the passage from childhood to adulthood, the new harvest, the hunting season, etc. Many distinct styles reflect the diversity of the Angolan cultural tradition."

Benin

BENIN—Jane Rodgers, Fitzgerald, Georgia

"Red, green, and yellow are the colors of the flag of Benin. The spiral design was adapted from a traditional basket design. It can also represent the unique music of modern Benin, which is a fusion of native music with American, French, Ghanian, and Congolese influences. The leopard is from Benin's coat of arms."

Botswana

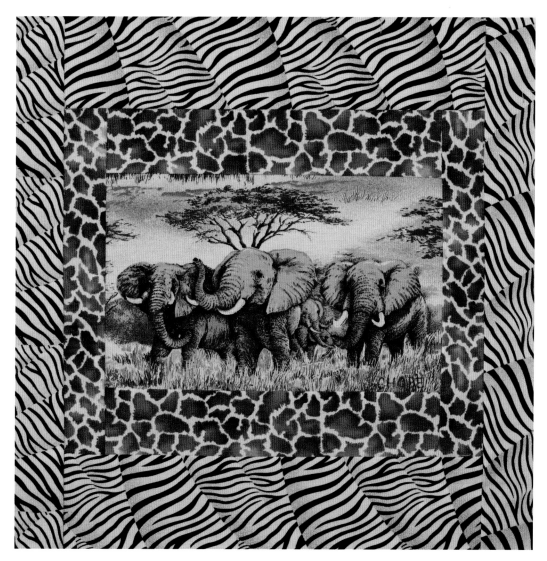

BOTSWANA—Brenda Shelby, Atlanta, Georgia

"While on safari in Chobe National Park in Botswana, I had the opportunity to see giraffes, elephants, and zebras in the wild with my own eyes—some of my favorite animals! I had to include this magical experience in my block. Botswana is comprised largely of plains and grasslands, and national parks such as Chobe provide a refuge for these beautiful but endangered creatures that for many people have come to symbolize Africa's wildlife and natural beauty."

BURKINA FASO—Sarah Ridgeway*, Atlanta, Georgia

"The primitive construction of this block represents the indigenous African heritage of my ancestors. Had it been done as it was in their time, there would be different fabrics in the dark and light patches of the block. This is my attempt to create an original design that had a primitive feel to connect to the people of Burkina Faso."

Burundi

BURUNDI—Wanda Hickman*, Dunwoody, Georgia

"Burundi is a small, landlocked country in east central Africa. In 1993, Marguerite 'Maggy' Barankitse saved twenty-five children from slaughter during the worst year of Burundi's civil war. She started a home for orphaned children, a former schoolhouse she named *Maison Shalom* (House of Peace). Since then, she and her team have opened many children's villages. These 500 small houses provide children the support and nurturing they need by reintegrating them with loving families. This quilt block is dedicated to Maggy, her team, and all her children."

Cameroon

CAMEROON—Meg Latimer, Alpharetta, Georgia

"Silhouetted against a traditional pieced star block in the colors of the flag are three of Cameroon's native species. Several kinds of antelope, including the Bushbuck, Sui, Roan, and Sitatunga are indigenous to Cameroon. The Sitatunga hides from its predators by submerging itself underwater with only its nose exposed like a snorkel. Both the black and white rhino are found in Cameroon, both having poor eyesight but an excellent sense of smell and acute hearing. The giraffe, which has excellent eyesight and sense of smell, is found there as well. Measuring 6 feet at birth, it towers over everyone. You wouldn't want to try to keep up with a giraffe—its stride measures 15 feet!"

Cape Verde

CAPE VERDE—Marian Garber*, Lake Park, Georgia

Sun Over Cape Verde

"Cape Verde is a country of islands located off the coast of West Saharan Africa. The name means, of course, 'green cape', and I chose to represent this in my color palette. Peaceful as these elegant green peaks may seem, the islands are rugged and many storms that develop into hurricanes originate here. The islands are a popular refueling stop for air and sea traffic."

CENTRAL AFRICAN REPUBLIC—Cleme Crosby, Fayetteville, Georgia

"In the fall, butterflies fill the sky as if it were snowing. When they die, people gather them up and make butterfly art. This is why I chose the butterfly to represent the Central African Republic."

Chad

CHAD—Carolyn Powers, Roswell, Georgia

"The sun represents the extremely hot temperatures (in excess of 120 degrees Fahrenheit in the summer). The land is very dry, hence the desert-like colors for the earth, with an occasional acacia tree (except in the southernmost part of Chad where it is wetter and more fertile). There is a mountainous region in the northwest, represented by the mountain on the left. The population is quite young, thus the young women and the baby. The people live simple lives, with limited electricity, and have difficulty obtaining water. The huts are typical of Chad. The women carry heavy loads and water on their heads and wear colorful clothing."

Comoros

COMOROS—Brenda Wade, Lawrenceville, Georgia

"The three pools of lava below the active volcano on Comoros' main island of Njazidja (or Grande Comore) represent the other three main islands of Comoros. The Comoros archipelago is located in the Indian Ocean off the east coast of Africa, between Mozambique and Madagascar. It is the world's second largest producer of vanilla, and is an increasingly popular tourist destination where visitors can enjoy the extensive beaches, the deep sea fishing or perhaps a hike to volcanic craters."

Democratic Republic of the Congo

DEMOCRATIC REPUBLIC OF THE CONGO—Sissy Anderson*, Lithonia, Georgia

"The top left square represents the sun, which is always shining upon the DRC. Depicted in the top right is a diamond—the DRC is the world's second largest producer of diamonds, primarily industrial diamonds. Blue represents the Congo River, which runs through the country, enabling thick forests to grow. My block was paper pieced in sections."

Republic of the Congo

REPUBLIC OF THE CONGO—Mary Maynard, Atlanta, Georgia

"I chose to make the Congo block because my mother was born in this country, then known as Belgian Congo. In trying to decide how to depict Congo, I talked to my mother, read my grandfather's book about his life there, and heard a story on NPR radio about Congo. My mother's first comment was about the river, and the NPR story discussed how the Congo River is still the highway of the country. Thus, I decided to depict life on the Congo River."

Côte d'Ivoire

The labels visible within the quilt: CÔTE D'IVOIRE, AFRICA · CONSERVATION · EDUCATION · REFORESTATION · AGRICULTURE · TEXTILES · COTTON · PETROLEUM · COFFEE · COCOA · WILDLIFE · FOREST

CÔTE D'IVOIRE—Alice Schriber*, Woodbury, Georgia

"Côte d'Ivoire is a West African country just a few degrees north of the equator, and is thus very sunny. Here can be found dense tropical forests, mountains and savannah. There is a large timber industry, and Côte d'Ivoire is the world's largest exporter of cocoa. Large herds of elephants once roamed the country. Unfortunately, their numbers have dwindled and they are now found almost exclusively in one preserve, which is shared with eastern neighbor, Ghana. I have tried to express Côte d'Ivoire's diverse geography, people, animals, and economy in the traditional nine-patch block form."

179

Djibouti

DJIBOUTI—Leslie Boone*, Lilburn, Georgia

"The name of this block representing Djibouti is Marathon. Since the recipient of my Olympic Quilt was a marathon runner (indeed, I think most if not all of the Djibouti team members were long distance runners), it seemed like a good choice. The brown in the center represents the arid climate, whereas the strips of color along the outside represent the vibrant and colorful culture."

Egypt

EGYPT—Helga Diggelmann, Alpharetta, Georgia

"The first things that come to mind when you think of Egypt are the pyramids. The traditional 'Moon Over the Mountain' block represents one of the great pyramids as seen from across the Nile, with a felucca in the foreground sailing quietly by."

EQUATORIAL GUINEA—Sandy Henry*, Dahlonega, Georgia

"Despite its name, I was astonished to learn that no part of Equatorial Guinea lies on the equator! I created this compass rose using the colors of the flag to represent this West African country. Although Equatorial Guinea has the smallest population of any African country and the third smallest land mass, it is the third largest oil producer in sub-Saharan Africa."

Eritrea

ERITREA—Renee Allen, Ellenwood, Georgia

"The art of personal adornment is one of the oldest and most widely practiced in human history, and the women of Eritrea have surely mastered it. This kind of facial decoration, accomplished with headbands, earrings, and multiple facial piercings is a traditional art form. I like to think that my pretty lady could be featured on the cover of *Vogue* as readily as on the cover of *National Geographic!*"

Ethiopia

ETHIOPIA—Mary Ruth McDonald, Roswell, Georgia

"Ethiopia's flag provided inspiration for fabric color selection and design. A country boundary silhouette in blue is appliquéd to a striped tricolor combination of green, yellow, and red background. Ethiopia has a history of gold medals in Olympic track and field events, so a figure of a running man embroidered in yellow thread completes the design."

GABON—Shirley Rathkopf*, Seattle, Washington

"Eighty-five percent of Gabon is covered in tropical rain forest, and its economy is driven by off-shore oil production. My husband used to carry oil products on his ship (he is a retired ship's captain), and that's why I chose Gabon. You can see little oil wells in the block, as well as different shades of green in the forest, crazy-patch style."

Gambia

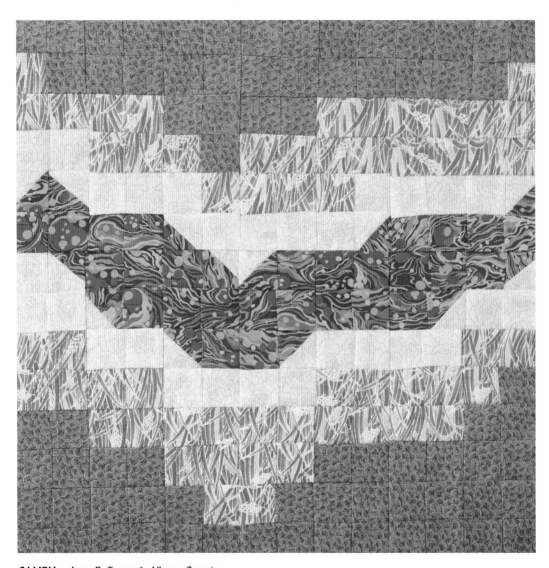

GAMBIA—Anne B. Townes*, Albany, Georgia

"The blue section through the middle of the block echoes the shape of Gambia, which is a narrow strip along the Gambia River, completely surrounded by Senegal. Using materials that I had on hand, I thought of the other strips as sand, reeds, and groundnuts (peanuts), which provide ninety percent of Gambia's export income."

Ghana

GHANA—Nancy DeCreny Franklin, Ellenwood, Georgia

"The beautiful handmade batiks used in this block were purchased on my first trip to Ghana in 2010. The stool is recognized as one reserved for tribal chieftains in the southern part of the country; the central motif, the adinkra symbol Gye Nyame, means "Only God." It is a symbol of the Asante people of southern Ghana, one of Ghana's many ethnic groups, and is seen throughout that area."

Guinea

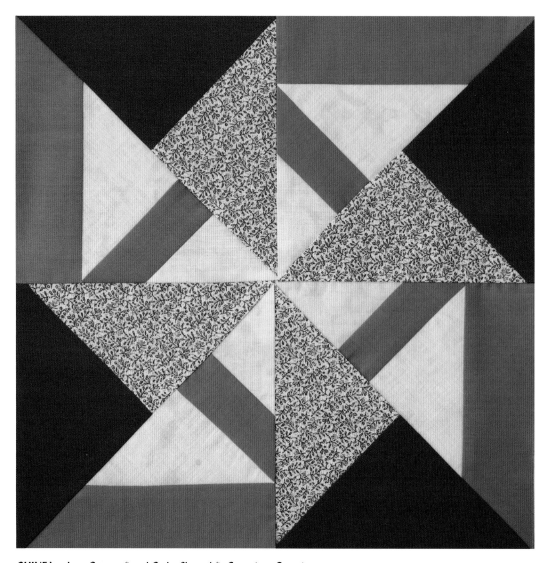

GUINEA—Jane Grayson* and Cathy Skrypek*, Cumming, Georgia

"The principal natural resources of Guinea are bauxite, iron ore, diamonds, and gold, here represented by the smaller, yellow pinwheel. Its agriculture forms the green background of the block. Each triangle of the larger pinwheel represents one of the primary ethnic groups: the Peuhl, the Malinke, the Soussous, and the Gerze/Toma."

188

Guinea-Bissau

GUINEA-BISSAU—Carol Larimer*, New Bern, North Carolina

"Guinea-Bissau, on the Atlantic coast of West Africa, is one of the world's least developed countries. As a quilt maker, I am aware that one element of the creative process is expression through a fabric's color and texture. Red-feathered pinwheels provide an African mood; gold fabric triangles symbolize cashew nuts—Guinea Bissau's main harvest!"

Kenya

KENYA—Eileen Sullivan, Duluth, Georgia

"Kenya is home to many of the world's top long distance runners and it dominates all other countries in these endurance events. I imagine the gifted Kenyan athletes striving for their personal best and giving everything they have to obtain Gold. The colors of the flag were another inspiration for this block. This country has a special place in my heart since my son worked there after graduate school, teaching video editing. He shared his wonderful experiences and photos with me."

Lesotho

LESOTHO—Linda Campbell*, Lawrenceville, Georgia

"This block was inspired by pictures of dwellings in Lesotho villages. I was particularly charmed by the bright blue doors of many of the houses."

Liberia

LIBERIA—Betsy Podriznik, Lawrenceville, Georgia

"This block was made to honor a wonderful and loving Liberian caregiver—Chris Pratt. While researching Liberia, I discovered a tie to quilting in the person of Martha Ann Ricks. Liberia has a long, rich history in textile arts and quilting. The free and former U.S. slaves who emigrated to Liberia brought with them their sewing and quilting skills. One of the best known Liberian quilters was Martha Ann Ricks (formerly of Tennessee and Virginia), who presented a quilt featuring the famed Liberian coffee tree to Queen Victoria of England in 1892. My block features a photo of Ms. Ricks, depicts the natural and cultural treasures of the country, and is bordered by the names of all the counties of Liberia."

Libya

LIBYA—O.V. Brantley, Atlanta, Georgia

"My vision of Libya is that of a country dominated by a harsh, relentless desert. However, I know that even in such a place, there is beauty. That is why my block features an oasis in the middle of the desert. I always look for a silver lining in every place, in every situation, and in every person."

Madagascar

MADAGASCAR—Irene McLaren*, Miami, Florida

"Madagascar is comprised of mountains and desert, and is surrounded by ocean. When I think of Madagascar, I think of sea, sand, and mountains. I have tried to convey this in my block, which also incorporates the colors of the flag—red, green, and white."

Malawi

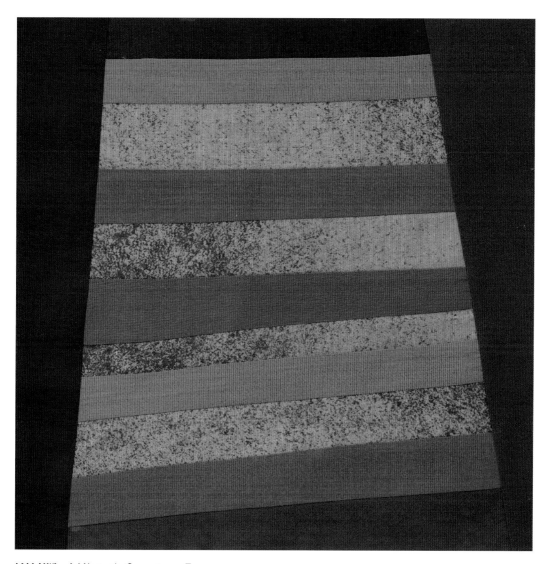

MALAWI—Jul Kamen*, Georgetown, Texas

"From my study of African textiles, art, and music, I have learned that one of the most significant characteristics of the culture is *improvisation*. It is not common for an exact design or pattern to be replicated over and over verbatim; rather, an idea or sketch serves as a starting point from which variations are made in a highly personal or unique way. Colors are traditionally high-contrast (dark against light) and 'clashing' or complementary. My block is a 'string-style' block with a crazy, log-cabin border."

Mali

MALI—Linda Campbell*, Lawrenceville, Georgia

"In creating this block, I was inspired by motifs used in the traditional bogolanfini mud cloth designs indigenous to Mali. I combined checkerboard, stripes, and hourglass shapes in a four-block unit that is repeated four times and set by rotating the four units to create the overall design. These four-block units were paper pieced and then assembled. These units can be rotated in many ways for a variety of looks. Different color choices can completely change the look as well."

Mauritania

MAURITANIA—Kathy Oppelt, Lawrenceville, Georgia

"The color of sand is similar to the color of the camel—I imagined camels that would blend into to the sand, with a great, peaceful stillness to the surroundings ... perhaps only the sound of the sighing wind disturbing the silence of the desert."

Mauritius

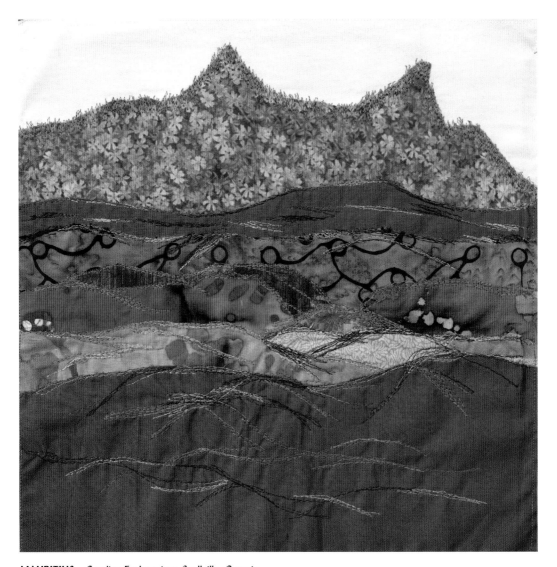

MAURITIUS—Carolina Fuchssteiner, Snellville, Georgia

"What could be more beautiful than a place where the colors of the dirt from volcanoes change as if they were made of batik fabrics spread out on the ground? My block depicts the unique colors of the sands of Chamarel on the island of Mauritius."

Morocco

MOROCCO—Designed by Carla Zahl Jolman*, Muskegon, Michigan; made by Peggy Turner*, Valdosta, Georgia

Moroccan Rug

"Morocco is located on the northwestern coast of Saharan Africa. It is an ancient country with a rich cultural heritage. The traditional rug patterns of Morocco were the inspiration for this design. The hot colors are reminiscent of the blazing desert sun."

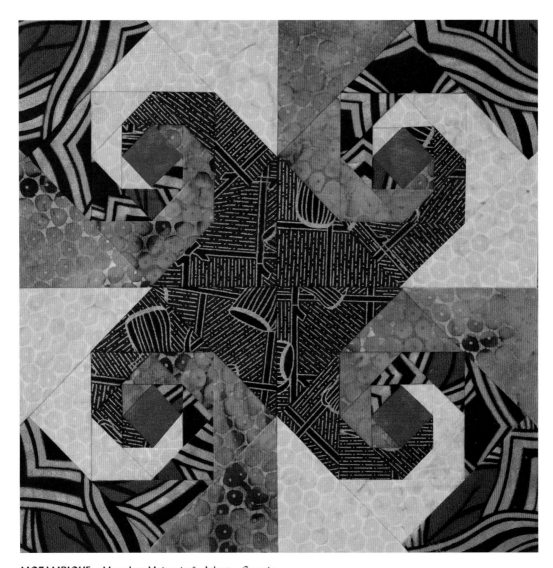

MOZAMBIQUE—Mary Lou Mojonnier*, Atlanta, Georgia

"This variation of the traditional 'Snail's Trail' block represents the elephants of the Maputo Elephant Reserve. The colorful and brightly patterned fabrics used represent the strong and vibrant culture of Mozambique."

NAMIBIA—Shirley Rathkopf*, Seattle, Washington

"The diamond industry is one of Namibia's most important sources of revenue, so I wanted my block to reflect this precious gemstone. As you can see, I rendered the diamond in soft gold tones, but then projected its refraction pattern in the brown and reddish tones of the background fabric."

NIGER—Renee Allen, Ellenwood, Georgia

Nomads of Niger

"In Niger it is the men who embellish and adorn themselves to attract women. The man of Niger I've created wears earrings, a necklace, a fancy hat, and facial decoration as signs of his prosperity and desirability."

Nigeria

NIGERIA—Marva Swanson, Atlanta, Georgia

"I find inspiration for creating quilts in a variety of unique items, but I particularly love African masks. They embrace the mystical tradition of an entire culture and highlight physical and spiritual elements of indescribable beauty. I consider them among the most fantastic works of African art as well as a subtle documentation of the continent's history. I felt an emotional connection to the beautiful royal Bini mask—as one of Nigeria's most renowned masks, it is as recognizable as it is revered. My interpretation unites elements of the mask and the region it represents. I used a sheer, transparent silk fabric with a green and white border; the silk symbolizes the veil between two worlds while the colors in the border, embellished with green crystals and green shells, represent the Nigerian flag."

Rwanda

RWANDA—Akiko Matsumoto, Atlanta, Georgia

"The name of this block is 'Voices.' The woman has her lips slightly open, perhaps to speak or to smile. I read that there are some female politicians in Rwanda and that one of the crafts of the area is basket making. I purchased a very beautiful basket made in Rwanda here in Atlanta, Georgia. The women's voices are reaching here. And I hope my craft will reach someone's heart, as the unknown maker's beautiful basket touched mine."

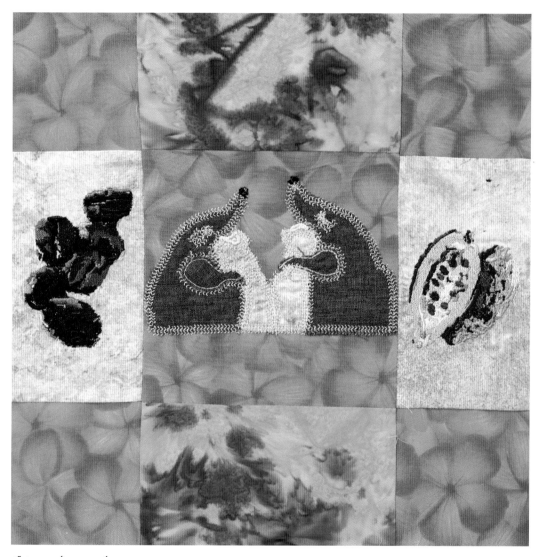

SÃO TOMÉ AND PRÍNCIPE—Kathy McGill, Beaufort, SC

"Brilliant colors represent the ocean, greenery, and beaches of this island nation. Shown in the center are the adorable São Tomé shrews, which are unique to the island. The coffee beans and cocoa beans that grow on these islands complete my portrait of São Tomé and Príncipe."

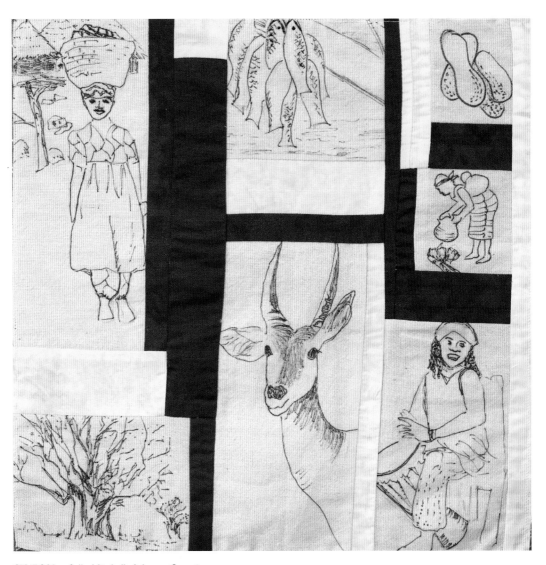

SENEGAL—Sally Mitchell, Atlanta, Georgia

"Senegal is a remarkable country with beautiful people who have a strong work ethic and buoyant spirits in a setting of ocean, desert, cities, and remote villages. Several scenes of Senegalese village life are depicted in pen and ink in my block."

SEYCHELLES—Helga Diggelmann, Alpharetta, Georgia

"The Seychelles coat of arms includes a sailfish. This stylized version of the 'flying fish' incorporates a traditional 'flying geese' motif. The fish also reflects the colors of the Seychelles flag."

SIERRA LEONE—Ruth McKinley*, Morganton, Georgia

"Since Sierra Leone means Lion Mountains, I decided to depict both in my block—a lion and the mountains! To its credit, Sierra Leone has the reputation of being a country that shows no discrimination between tribes, people or religions."

Somalia

SOMALIA—Nicole Blackwell, Ellenwood, Georgia

"Culturally, life in Somalia centers around family and the strict adherence to religious practices. The Somali women of this block honor these traditions by customarily covering their heads, signifying modesty. Like the Somali flag, the beautiful blue background and the star overhead suggest the Somali sky and African freedom, respectively."

SOUTH AFRICA—Helga Diggelmann, Alpharetta, Georgia

"South Africa is the land of my birth. It is a complex nation of many different people groups. This uneven nine patch block represents the various ethnic backgrounds, superimposed by the colors from the South African flag."

South Sudan

SOUTH SUDAN—Renee Allen, Ellenwood, Georgia

"Africa's newest country, South Sudan is rich in oil deposits yet experiences unpredictable rainfall and water shortages. These women wear traditional dress—the long, flowing robes that shield them from the sun and which also add a bit of color to an otherwise harsh landscape. One woman carries a pot on her head in the traditional manner. Subsistence in the inhospitable Sudanese climate is a continual challenge for these nomadic people."

Sudan

SUDAN—Renee Allen, Ellenwood, Georgia

"Sudan is rich with the antiquity of the pyramids and the Nile River basin. The domed buildings represent centers of commerce, which are located at the confluence of the blue Nile and the white Nile. I used upholstery cloth to achieve the desired texture of the rugged, unforgiving desert environment."

Swaziland

SWAZILAND—Dora White, Conyers, Georgia

"The giraffe's natural predator is the lion, but its most dangerous predator is man, who seeks the giraffe for its meat, its hide, and its long, black tail hairs. As a result, it is becoming far less abundant in the wild and is now only somewhat safe within game parks and sanctuaries. Several of these are found in Swaziland. The design of my block was inspired by ancient petroglyphs found in sub-Saharan Niger."

Tanzania

TANZANIA—Audrey Hiers*, Blairsville, Georgia

"Although *all* of Tanzania is impressive, to me a real standout of this spectacular country is Mount Kilimanjaro, and *nothing* man-made can compare. This is my folk art appliquéd interpretation of this majestic mountain."

Togo

TOGO—Elisa Woods, Atlanta, Georgia

"Togo is in West Africa, bordered by Ghana to the west, Benin to the east, and Burkina Faso to the north. Togo was part of slave trade and the central image of my block depicts the people captured and the tears shed during this period. My base block colors, green and yellow, are found in the country's flag."

Tunisia

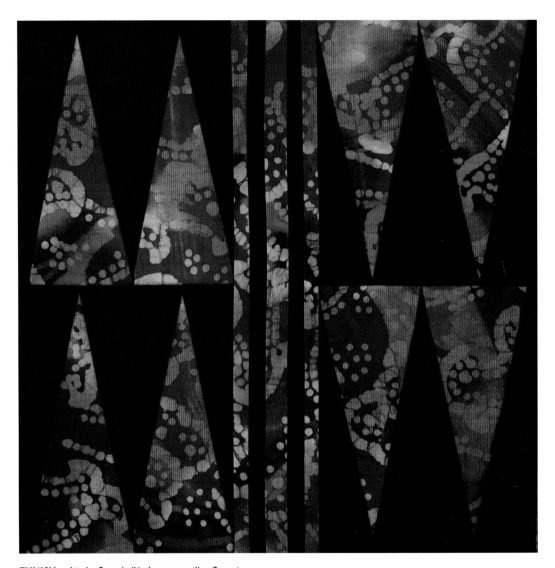

TUNISIA—Linda Campbell*, Lawrenceville, Georgia

"This block was inspired by a woven Tunisian textile that features strips of thin triangles and decorative stripes set in a field of red wool. My block features sets of large triangles running up and down each side to add interest and flexibility to the setting of the block. I created the triangle units using the paper piecing technique, although they could also be created using templates."

Uganda

UGANDA—Holly Anderson*, Cumming, Georgia

"The rich textile tradition of Uganda and the Ugandan peoples' love of vibrant colors are reflected in this design. Many of the motifs used in woven and printed textiles reflect the Ugandans' respect for nature, often portrayed, as here, in a folk art style."

Zambia

ZAMBIA—Nicole Blackwell, Stone Mountain, Georgia

"Elephants are among the most graceful creatures found along the Zambezi River in southern Africa's Zambia. They symbolize the untamed nature of Zambia's wildlife, the quiet beauty of its land, and the enduring strength of its people. Although hunted to endangerment for their precious tusks, these animals are crucial to the preservation of wildlife in the Zambezi Valley. My quilt block, with the traditional log cabin in the background, depicts the stirring of these gentle giants as the sun rises over the land and the day begins."

Zimbabwe

ZIMBABWE—Brenda Shelby, Atlanta, Georgia

"The Victoria Falls impressed me on my trip to Zimbabwe … so much water with so much power! The blue and white fabric helped me to convey the sense of thundering force of the world's largest curtain of water. I surrounded the falls with leaves using the dimensional appliqué technique to depict the lush, green setting of this world heritage site."

Index

*indicates maker of Olympic or Paralympic quilt